. . 'I DO'

. . 'I DO'

Your Guide to a Happy Marriage

Hans J Eysenck

with
Betty Nichols Kelly

CENTURY PUBLISHING
LONDON
&
MULTIMEDIA PUBLICATIONS (UK) LIMITED

This book was devised and produced by
Multimedia Publications (UK) Ltd

Editor: Christopher Fagg
Production: Arnon Orbach
Design: Mike Spike
Illustration: Rosemary Harrison
Diagrams: Shirley Wheeler

First published in Great Britain in 1983
by Century Publishing Co. Ltd, 76 Old Compton Street, London W1,
and Multimedia Publications (UK) Ltd, Central House,
1 Ballards Lane, London N3

ISBN 0 7126 0008 6

B/W origination by D.S. Colour International Ltd, London
Typeset by Wyvern Typesetting Ltd, Bristol, and
printed in Great Britain by
Butler & Tanner Ltd, Frome and London

Contents

To Sybil, of course!

Introduction

Marriage, despite rumours of its imminent demise, remains one of our most popular institutions. Moreover, marriage is good for us. According to all the most recent studies, married people are happier, healthier and have more self-esteem than their single counterparts. They tend to live longer and, in general, have a more positive outlook on life.

If marriage is so good for us, how does it happen that so many marriages are filled with unhappiness? Why do one in three couples get divorced? And how can we reconcile this high rate of divorce with the idea of marriage as a popular institution?

The answers to these questions are far from simple, but I feel that much of the problem springs from inappropriate selection of marriage partners. My research shows that, of all the factors that make for success or failure in marriage, it is the question of personality that is crucial. And the assessment of personality is an area of which most people are, understandably, comparatively ignorant. Many marriages, then, are doomed – or at least destined for severe growing pains right from the start.

My hope, in writing this book, is that the insights gained by psychology can help people understand more about themselves, so that when the time comes to choose a mate they will be able to make a fairly good job of it.

Much of what I have to say is based on my own research in the fields of personality, sex and marriage. In my study on happiness and satisfaction in marriage, 560 married couples agreed to fill out detailed questionnaires about their marital happiness, their personalities, their sexual attitudes and behaviour and their social attitudes. These volunteers came from all walks of life. They were solicited through newspaper and magazine advertisements, and I was very careful to make sure that they answered the questionnaires independently from their spouses, and that they sent in their answers without knowing what their spouses said. Although these couples did not represent a random sample of the population, when I compared their answers to the questions for which national norms were available, little difference emerged.

Since none of the people in this group were divorced I used the data collected by Thornes and Collard for their book *Who Divorces?* They studied 331 female and 180 male divorcés, as well as 354 married women and 193 married men. They used my personality inventories and I was able to analyze the results and apply it to what I had learned about married couples.

I also relied on a series of my studies of sex and personality which used 800 male and female students, 850 adult males and females from 18 to 60 with an average age of 30, and a group of 500 male and female twins. This last provided valuable insights into the genetic factors which determine sexual attitudes and behaviour. Again, using identical and fraternal twins, I conducted a study of how happiness and unhappiness are determined by personality and by genetic and environmental factors. It is this last study that has provided me with the findings most relevant to this book.

What, then, do I intend to do in a book about happiness in marriage? Certainly I offer no quick and easy solutions to the subtle stresses that exist between married couples. One of the major findings of modern psychology is that each individual differs from all other individuals in countless important ways, so that what is sauce for the goose is by no means sauce for the gander. Advice suitable for an introvert may be quite inappropriate for an extravert; what may be true for the solid, emotionally stable person may be quite untrue for the more mercurial, less stable person.

All I can really do is to tell you, factually, what is known about this subject. Science can give the facts about marriage and how they are related to such concepts as intelligence, personality and social and sexual behaviours. But it is up to you to decide how to apply these to your own life.

If different people need different things and react differently to the same circumstances, how then are you going to be able to interpret what I say? You must make an effort to get to know yourself, and what your reactions are likely to be. To help you do this, I have included many questionnaires about personality, attitudes, and happiness, as well as the questionnaire about marital happiness used in our studies. By answering these questionnaires you should be able to get a rough idea of where you stand on these issues. It is in this spirit of 'know thyself' that these questionnaires are intended. They can help you understand just what psychologists mean by the terms introversion versus extraversion, emotional stability versus instability, and high libido versus low libido. The questionnaires can give you a fairly clear idea of how you compare with other people when it comes to these qualities. You will then be in a position to apply this information to the general findings in the book.

With luck, you'll be able to get a better idea of just how much free choice you have, and how much of your behaviour is influenced by genetic factors. It would be silly of me to tell a poor, uneducated man that by reading this book he would be able to make an impression on a Farah Fawcett or a Brooke Shields; it would be equally unreasonable to promise a volatile, unstable individual that by reading this book he or she will escape the anxieties that make his or her life unhappy. Certain things can be done to make one's life happier, but there are no magic formulae, and it would be irresponsible of a social scientist to suggest that there are. We must recognize the limitations of our knowledge and learn how to be as effective as we can within those limitations.

Neither the social nor the physical scientists have the answers to all of our questions. The psychologist studying marriage is trying to understand how two very complex entities, a man and a woman, interact, and how much of this interaction is determined by their personality, intelligence, environment, age, and experience. This is no easy task, particularly since he is unable to manipulate the people involved experimentally, for obvious reasons. Compare the problems faced by the social scientist with those of the physicist who is trying to understand, let's say, the way two water molecules interact when they collide. The physicist has the great advantage of controlling the units involved in his experiment, and certainly those units are much less complex than a human being. Nevertheless, Felix Franks, one of the great authorities on the study of water, has said, 'After spending large sums of money on computer time we are not very much nearer to understanding how even *two* water molecules interact when they collide; nor do we know the mechanism by which many water molecules interact to form *ordinary* liquid water.' This may give you a better idea of the difficulties faced by the psychologist, and how important it is for him not to claim too much for his hard-won knowledge. The science of human relationships is imperfect at best, but we can gain from it some general guidelines, together with certain assumptions which do tend to hold up over time.

Yet, there is a certain confusion about some of the popular hypotheses concerning marriage. For example, many people hold to the proposition that marriages are happiest when like marries like, while many others believe in the old theory that 'opposites attract'. General statements like these can certainly be investigated scientifically, and later on in this book we shall see to what extent one or other is true. There are other assumptions which have been tested, and it seems to me that at least some of the results reached are fairly definitive, at least for our Western culture. These, too, I shall examine in more detail.

As I indicated earlier, I firmly believe that, despite its ups and downs, marriage is even more popular now than it was sixty years ago. True, there are more divorces, but 80 per cent of the people who are getting divorced promptly remarry. Furthermore, as I've already mentioned, married people are healthier and happier than those who are single, separated, widowed or divorced. Marriage is no cure-all, but it does have a very positive effect on most of us.

Those who attack marriage for its imperfections fail to notice that they are measuring it by the wrong yardstick. We should not measure any human institution against perfection, but against available alternatives. By this standard, marriage emerges as an institution which has stood the test of time and holds up very well against every alternative life-style. In a good marriage, both the man and the woman are able to nurture feelings of intimacy, security and trust that lead to high self-esteem and general stability. In my opinion, intimacy is the key, the kind of intimacy that is only achieved when two people know, understand and care about each other deeply and sincerely. Such intimacy generates a sense of uniqueness, even exclusiveness, within a relationship which powerfully compensates for the sacrifice, by both partners, of the possibility of exciting new lovers. When it comes to happiness and contentment of people in general, marriage in some form or other has been the solution for all known societies.

I think it is important here for me to mention a word or two about my own experience with marriage. Having gone through one moderately unhappy marriage, and enjoying now a very happy one, I feel that I do have some knowledge of the pros and cons of marriage. There was a time when I was inclined to agree with those who claimed that it was insane to expect anyone to live in a monogamous state for any length of time with another person. No longer. I now think that long, mutually fulfilling, happy marriages can and do exist, and I have witnessed a fair number. This, of course, does not prove that marriage is the most desirable state for all people. Certainly there are some who are better off unmarried. On the whole, however, the evidence suggests that marriage has many more advantages than disadvantages, and this alone will ensure the survival of marriage in one form or another.

One final word. This book has been written from the point of view of empirical science. By 'empirical' I simply mean based on the facts as observed. I do not intend to pass any moral, religious or ethical judgments on the findings I discuss.

Certainly you are free to view anything I have to say from your own religious or ethical perspective. Science has little to say about such issues, and I avoid them here, because I am presenting my findings as a psychologist and social scientist, not as a philosopher.

As the Earl of Chesterfield once said: 'In matters of religion I never give any advice, because I will not have anybody's torments in this world or the next laid to my charge.' Nothing in this book should be construed as advice in any direct sense. Use my insights and suggestions as you will and, although I make no promises, I sincerely hope that they will improve your chances for marital happiness and fulfilment. However, the study of human behaviour, especially as we watch its interaction in marriage, is certainly an imperfect science. Science itself does not know all the answers, but outside science there are no answers. So, take what you can from what I have to offer, and prosper.

H. J. Eysenck
Institute of Psychiatry
University of London, 1982

1

Are marriages made in heaven?

One was never married, and that's his hell;
another is, and that's his plague.

DEMOCRITUS

Marriage is universal. Every human society has had its various forms: *monogamy*, or single-partner marriage (although our present divorce rate suggests that *serial monogamy* – a series of single-partner marriages – is the modern trend); or *polygamy* (such as practised by early-day Mormons and even some contemporary followers of Muhammad), the latter with its two distinct forms, *polygyny*, one man with many wives, and the rarer *polyandry*, a woman with more than one husband. Polygyny, of course, has been the most common form of polygamy, and historically it has extended not only to the possession of many wives by a man of great influence and wealth; it really goes back into our very evolutionary roots, a 'harem condition' encountered sporadically throughout the animal kingdom. (Keep in mind, however, that the women's liberation movement is young; who knows what the future will bring!) Whatever its form, marriage seems to be an integral part of the human condition, and it probably has been with us for well over ten thousand years.

Why, then, despite its universal appeal, is marriage so controversial? Why is it a topic that brings comments ranging from the wildly enthusiastic to the profoundly sceptical? 'There is no more lovely, friendly, and charming relationship, communion, or good company than a good marriage', Martin

Luther said. 'Marriage is like life in this – that it is a field of battle, and not a bed of roses', argued Robert Louis Stevenson. Every argument for marriage has an equal counterpart for its rejection, and the fact that divorce rates are rising while weddings are also on the increase only seems to make it a draw. So why on earth do people marry?

Every person throughout written history has had something different to say about marriage, but on one thing all agree:

Drawings by Charles Addams © New Yorker Magazine 1975

'We're not living happily ever after.'

marriage is viewed differently by men and women. 'Who so findeth a wife, findeth a good thing', says the Bible. Perhaps so, but Bertrand Russell had this to say: 'Marriage is for women the commonest mode of livelihood, and the total amount of undesired sex endured by women is probably greater in marriage than in prostitution.' On the other hand, Lord Byron felt that, 'Man's love is of man's life a thing apart, 'Tis woman's whole existence'. 'Every woman should marry – and no man', declared Disraeli. Predictably, Oscar Wilde found marriage a rich source of contradiction: 'Men marry because they are tired; women because they are curious; both are disappointed.'

While I don't agree with the cynical Wilde, this book does operate on the assumption that men and women are not the same. There are innate and societally-induced differences that may not control but certainly do influence us, and they must be recognized – not only in order to enjoy a happy marriage, but to select the right partner in the first place. That is the subject of this book.

Monogamy or monotony?

The Victorians went too far when they said that men marry in order to have sex but women have sex in order to marry, but this fundamental relationship between sex and marriage does get to the essence of the contradiction within the marital state: marriage offers us a steady supply of what appears to be most appealing in diversity. In the animal kingdom, this is known as the Coolidge Effect.

Once the former President visited a government farm with his wife. They were taken on separate tours of inspection, and when the First Lady passed the chicken pens she asked the guide how often each day the rooster would normally perform his duty. 'Dozens', was the answer. Most impressed, Mrs Coolidge asked the guide to 'Please tell that to the President'. Later on when the President passed the chicken pens and was told of the rooster's performance, he inquired whether the rooster performed each time with the same hen. 'A different one

17

each time', was the answer. 'Tell that to Mrs Coolidge', said the President.

This Coolidge Effect can be seen throughout the animal kingdom, and domesticated animals such as rams and bulls or experimental creatures such as rats have made it possible for scientists to study the phenomenon. In the case of the latter (I speak of rats, not scientists), the male will initially copulate a number of times but then tire of the female in his cage, becoming potent again only when a new one is supplied. In fact, a new lady rat will completely restore him to his former state of vigour. Unfortunate, if all too applicable, comparisons can occasionally be made among human beings: what marriage counsellor has not seen the husband impotent or lethargic with his wife but boundlessly amorous with his mistress(es)? However, keep in mind that, at least literally, men are not rats, and that this Coolidge Effect is very 'species-specific'. What is natural for rams and bulls is not a strong or even common instinct among the primates, including man. Furthermore, human beings consider factors other than sex important in

marriage, be they financial benefits, interest in children, or mutual support and comfort. All these and many more components make marriage a complex and difficult relationship.

Love and marriage

> *One should always be in love; that is*
> *the reason one should never marry.*
>   OSCAR WILDE

There is also that curious phenomenon we call 'love'. While it has certainly not been considered an essential ingredient in the arranged marriages found around the world, Western society (probably wealthy enough to afford the luxury of love) has come to believe that it is a necessary part of marriage. Unfortunately, it is ironic that love often seems to suffer the same fate as the sexual impulse; it is almost as if there were a Coolidge Effect for love as well that prevents it from surviving the first five years of marriage. Certainly the presence of love at the beginning of a marriage is no guarantee that it will endure.

Whence comes marriage?

In view of all the difficulties produced by marriage, and in the light of all the sceptical and hostile comments concerning it, it would seem that marriage could only exist because it is indeed almost part of our instinctual heritage. Perhaps the answer lies in our primate past.

From his observations of the Hamadryas baboons on Monkey Hill at the London Zoo, Professor Solly Zuckerman developed the hypothesis that the social unit of many monkey and ape societies is a family group consisting of a male overlord and a varying number of females and their young. This 'harem principle' operating among apes is a primitive, primate form of polygyny. It is clearly an established system, as well as the law of that particular jungle, for unmated males outside specified

19

harem groups obtain no sexual relief and are continuously trying to capture receptive females. However, monogamy itself may have its roots among the apes. Dorothy Cheney and Bob Seyfarth of the University of Cambridge followed baboons around southern Africa and found that adult males who had harems nevertheless developed preferences for one particular female, spending more time with her and herding her away from other males – this even when new, sexually receptive females were offered and the preferred one was unresponsive and lactating! Perhaps this is a rudimentary form of love.

It is very likely that our own *human* ancestors over the past four million years developed in a similar fashion. Certainly one

Drawing by Edward Koren © *New Yorker* Magazine 1975

'Are you a hunter or a food gatherer?'

can imagine the polygamous harem principle of 'marriage' operating; and Professor Zuckerman again suggests that monogamy was a natural, inevitable outgrowth of this. Why? *Because man became a hunter.* As the only carnivorous primate, early man would have to go out and hunt for food, an act that is difficult to perform for one female, let alone an entire harem. In a hunting regime, the male became responsible for providing food at a time when the female was too busy feeding and tending her baby to forage for herself. This 'duration of dependency' would have had a direct relation to the development of *male-female bonding* in early human communities. From a biological viewpoint, the need for the male to repress his wayward sexual impulses in the interests of male-female bonding was actually a necessary development for the survival of the species. It may sound contradictory, but in this way 'love' became the only practical answer, the mediator between the male's 'natural' promiscuity and tendency toward dominance and the social restraints put upon his sexual impulses for the sake of the female and the young. No wonder that thousands of years later it is still a shaky truce. Whether we like it or not, the battle between the sexes and women's fight for equality are both based on solid biological grounds. Fortunately for all of us, the ground was fertile for cultural developments that would lead first to polygamy and, eventually, to what surely can be called the more civilized form of marriage, monogamy.

Monogamy in other species

Male-female bonding, the true meaning of monogamy, is not a purely human phenomenon. Monogamous behaviour, in which at least one of the sexes typically copulates exclusively with one partner throughout at least one estrus or breeding season, can be found throughout the animal kingdom. Wolves, yellow-bellied marmots, snow buntings, European beavers, and Alaskan fur seals are all monogamous, as are certain other animals for which the mother's need for nourishment would otherwise interfere with her baby-tending. In these species the male's role is to gather food, or to protect the young for periods when the mother is foraging. As we have seen, in the human species, a male predilection for hunting only furthered this male-female division of labour. Eventually, such permanent or semi-permanent human unions inevitably became enshrined in social contracts. One of them, of course, is called marriage.

The dimorphic determinant

Monogamy can be *seen* as well as studied. Dimorphism, the degree to which males and females differ in size and shape, is much *less* pronounced in monogamous species whether animal or human. In other words, species with larger, stronger males tend to be polygynous, all the better to compete for more females. But there is even more significance beyond mere build, in the size of the testes. A large animal with smaller testes tends to be poly*gamous* but not promiscuous. In other words, he will mate with, but also guard and care for, a defined harem of females who will cooperate in sharing sexual favours according to their estruses. The male orangutan, for example, is half as big again as the female but has small testes. The naturally promiscuous male chimpanzee, on the other hand, has huge testes, making it easy for him to ejaculate with a number of females within the entire community.

So where do we put the human male? The masculine sex of *Homo sapiens* tends to have a build and testes size that place him somewhere between polygamy and monogamy, this uneasy compromise being responsible both for the attraction of marriage *and* the proliferation of divorce. There are sound reasons for the confusion and disagreements over the adequacy of the institution of marriage!

Biology or sociology?

The existence of this tension in the institution called marriage is itself a compromise between our biological and social natures. Indeed, we are neither but *both*. Man, or woman, is a *biosocial* animal, one influenced both by genetic inheritance and social customs. All too often biologists forget the importance of social precepts and modelling, while sociologists tend to ignore the importance of our biological inheritance. Both factors exercise control over our behaviour: social customs modify the expression of our biological urges, while chromosomally determined behaviour patterns may disrupt social rules which fail to accommodate them. Throughout this book I hope to adopt a biosocial perspective to help you choose your mate, and understand why you are doing so.

Is there life after marriage?

Is marriage dying as an institution? People have been predicting its demise for generations now, while those who raise their voices in the course of 'open' relationships have already pronounced it dead.

A look at the figures on pages 24 and 25 overleaf, however, does not suggest any such thing. While changes in the law and social pressures have lent themselves to more living-together arrangements as well as more divorces, new rulings have also made it easy to marry – and more people are doing so. In the United Kingdom, the Family Law Reform Act of 1969 lowered the age of consent from 21 to 18, thereby increasing the number of marriages; whereas the Divorce Reform Act freed many individuals to marry or remarry – which they have been doing at an increasing rate. This change

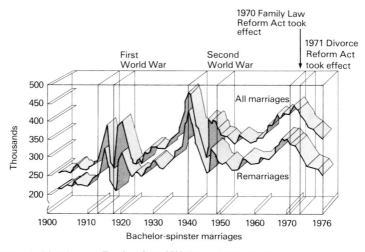

Figure 1: Marriages, England and Wales, 1900–1976

in legislation is probably responsible for the fact that by 1974 one out of four marriages included a divorced person. This general trend is true not only in Britain and the United States, but in other countries as well, despite regional differences in the duration of marriages.

The institution of marriage, then, seems to be holding its own. But, however we interpret the figures, the fact remains that divorce is on the increase. And because married people generally tend to be happier (and actually healthier) than single people, this book would like to see people stay within a good marriage. How to bring about this happy state of affairs is a different matter. A useful place to begin is the process of courtship itself. Is there any way of finding out whether your prospective partner will make a good, lasting mate? Many factors are involved, from a happy childhood for a possible spouse to economic security. And indeed hereditary traits themselves seem to be involved in a person's ability to form a happy union. This book will explore all areas, from the reason why wives seem to make the bigger adjustments (and why this

24

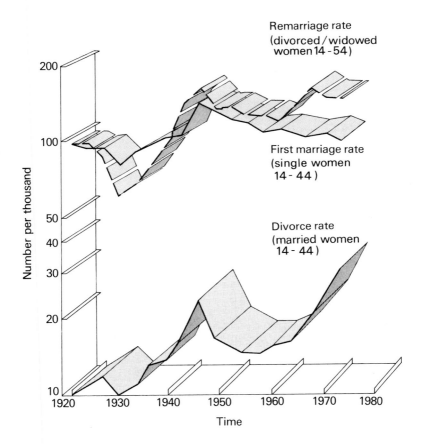

Figure 2: Rates of first marriage, divorce and remarriage among American women, 1920 to 1974. Each result is drawn from a sample of 1000 women aged 14–44 (first marriage and divorce) and 14–54 (remarriage).

may not necessarily be a bad thing), to how a person's intelligence and genetically determined 'Happiness Quotient' will affect both his or her choice and the marital aftermath. Marriage is a gamble under any circumstances; this book hopes to make the odds a little better for you.

Marriages – which ones are happy and what characterizes them?

According to sociologists only a fraction of successful and happy marriages fulfil the 'happy-ever-after' expectations envisaged by romantic films and novels. Such marriages – estimated at only 10 per cent of the total – are vastly outnumbered by those others which the experts have divided into three more or less self-explanatory groups. First is the *conflict* marriage. Characterized by constant bickering and arguing, this type of marriage by no means always leads to divorce. Indeed, many couples find the atmosphere of drama and confrontation mutually stimulating. Second comes the *devitalized* marriage, where couples seem bored with, or even indifferent to their partners, but nevertheless see their marriage as a good one and stay together. The third type of marriage is described as *passive-congenial*: here, responsibilities are shared in a civilized way and life is comfortable, without either of the couple seeming much bound up in the other. These three types, taken together, are described as *institutional*. The minority of so-called *companionship* marriages are divided into two types: *vital* marriages, where both partners are involved in every aspect of each other's lives, and *total* marriages, where the partners are so involved with each other that for them the outside world barely seems to exist at all.

The magic formula for creating and welding happy and enduring partnerships has so far eluded social scientists, though today they have more idea of what will *not* make for a happy marriage. The theory of opposites attracting, a phrase which trots off our tongues all too easily when attempting to explain a partnership where the protagonists appear to have nothing in common, seems to be breathing its last.

Of all the various qualities that might be extrapolated from a successful emotional relationship, *communication* seems the most significant. Seeing that marriage is now seen as a source of personal satisfaction rather than merely a business arrangement, this is what we might expect to find.

The main threats to effective communication include physical separation, being unwilling to talk about yourself or bad at interpreting your partner's needs and being on a 'different wavelength' from your partner, or failing to share his or her culture.

To be happy together marriage partners need not necessarily believe that the same things are important in life. What matters, researchers have found, is that they are able to compromise and show they respect the things their spouse values.

Researchers in Australia rated the happiness of 150 married couples and analysed the things the husbands and wives found important in life. They found that the happy couples did not necessarily share the same values.

What they did find was that people who see marriage as a means for their own satisfaction regardless of their spouse were less likely to be happily married, while an indicator of happiness in marriage is not so much sharing the same beliefs as the readiness to make concessions and accommodate one another.

Ref: C. E. Sharpley and J. A. Khan, Marital Adjustment, an Examination of some Predictive Variables, Psychological Reports, 1980, *47*, 379–82.

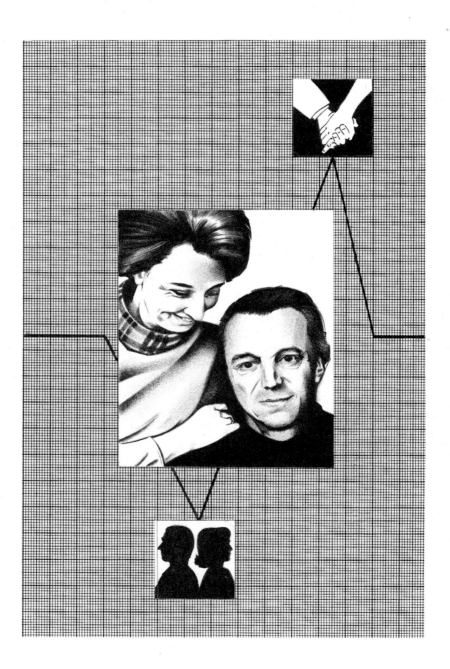

2

Happiness and the marital state

Despite the cynic's belief that the modern divorce courts prove that a 'happy marriage' is a contradiction in terms, the search for happiness is still one of the main reasons why people are continually looking for a mate. Marital bliss *means* happiness for them, and, because of that, a definition of happiness plays a key part in this book. But perhaps as far as marriage is concerned, the question is not 'what is happiness?' but *'who* is happy?'. Because the happiness and satisfaction to be found in marriage might very well be determined by the temperaments of those going into it. Is your prospective mate a happy person? Are *you* one? Is a Happiness Quotient (or HQ) part of an individual's personality profile? Happily, there are ways of finding answers to these questions.

Happiness and the individual

'Different men seek after happiness in different ways and by different means, and so make for themselves different modes of life', said Aristotle over 2 000 years ago. This diversity in men and women does not make scientific study of happiness impossible. On the contrary, studies have shown that no matter how different the ways in which people are questioned and interviewed, no matter what kinds of tests and questionnaires are given them, the results are remarkably similar. People who rate themselves happy by one method of research are usually similarly rated by other methods.

Happiness and sex differences

Taking the population as a whole, differences in general happiness between men and women are slight or non-existent; when we do observe them, however, they seem to favour women rather than men. Even this might be more a matter of appearance than reality because, whether women's feelings are the result of hormones or environment, our society allows women to show their emotions more, to *be* happy if they wish. The other side of the coin, of course, has women able to be unhappier as well: certainly, women do have higher levels of nervous breakdown, worry, anxiety, and other types of neurotic disorders. When marriage comes into the picture, however, clearer differences come to light. Studies show that both men and women are a great deal happier if married than if single, divorced, or widowed. However, single men were twice as likely as single women to rate themselves as 'not too happy'. The same holds true for divorced men and widowers. Divorced or widowed women are far happier than their male counterparts. Whether they care to admit it or not, the state of marriage *is* an important factor in men's happiness, and the difference in happiness between men and women in the married state is far less than in the single.

Does married happiness increase or decrease with age? For married women, it seems that happiness is at a constant level throughout their lives. One research project showed that 46 per cent of married women between the ages of 18 and 39 rated themselves happy, 46 per cent of those in the 40-to-59 year category did likewise, and 47 per cent of the married women over age 60 considered their state a happy one. The percentages for men, however, were startlingly different: 34 per cent, 40 per cent, and 44 per cent respectively, showing an increase of happiness with age. Perhaps men not only get older but wiser as well.

The complexity of happiness

We have said that people *express* their general level of happiness very consistently no matter which method of rating is used. But this still leaves the question as to whether we can find out the elements which go to make up the feeling of happiness or unhappiness. An intriguing study by Norman Bradburn may give us a clue. He began with the assumption that people added up the good things and feelings that they experienced, subtracted the bad things and feelings and reached an expressed level of happiness based on the difference.

He asked his respondents ten questions, five of them relating to positive feelings experienced during the past two weeks, the other five to negative ones. You might like to try the test yourself (see Tables 1 and 2).

31

Table 1

During the past two weeks did you ever feel:
(a)   pleased about having accomplished something
(b)   proud because someone complimented you on something you had done
(c)   particularly excited or interested in something
(d)   on top of the world
(e)   that things were going your way

or

(f)   bored
(g)   upset because someone criticized you
(h)   so restless that you couldn't sit long in a chair
(i)   very lonely or remote from other people
(j)   depressed or very unhappy

The answers were surprising!

Table 2

Percentage of respondents answering yes to both sets of questions:

(a)	84%	(f)	34%
(b)	71%	(g)	18%
(c)	54%	(h)	53%
(d)	33%	(i)	26%
(e)	71%	(j)	30%

Bradburn's assumption, of course, was that people who answered yes to the questions involving positive feelings would tend to say no to those involving negative feelings, and vice versa. In fact, no such simple relationship was found. At any one time, a person with many positive feelings may have many, or few, or an average number of negative feelings, and there seems to be no way at all of predicting one set of feelings by looking at the other. A person can be perfectly excited by one thing while being terribly depressed by something else going on in his or her life. Bradburn's study has shown us that we have two separate dimensions in life, what might be called a 'plus' and a 'minus' side. A person's plus range – called 'positive affect' – runs from high positive feelings to a lack of positive feelings altogether. By the same token, the minus side – 'negative affect' – extends from high negative feelings to a complete absence of them. Happiness, then, is a *compound* thing. The situation is rather as shown in Figure 4, where the happiness expressed is represented by the line running obliquely from top left to bottom right.

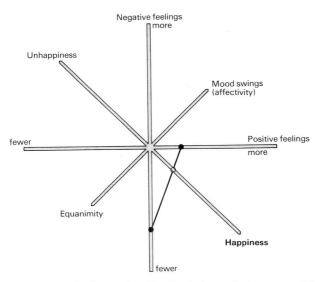

Figure 3: Happiness is determined by the balance between *positive* and *negative* feelings; these two classes of feelings are independent of each other. Rate yourself for your state of happiness at the moment: choose a position on the positive axis which roughly corresponds to the number of positive feelings you have. Now do the same on the negative axis for the number of negative feelings you have. Join the two points. The line will *either* cross the happiness dimension at a point indicating more or less happiness, *or* the dimension showing greater or lesser swings between moods of happiness and unhappiness.

Testing your Happiness Quotient

Would you like to test your own Happiness Quotient using Bradburn's test? Simply give a score of +1 for each yes answer to items (a) to (e), and a score of −1 for each yes answer to items (f) to (h). If you only score 0 or +1 in the plus column, please count it as 0. In the minus column, a score of −4 or −5 counts the same: record both as −4. You should now have a range of scores from 0 to 4 on each scale. If you then add your plus scores to your minus scores you'll get a single figure, ranging from −4 for very unhappy to +4 for very happy. Finally, to make all the scores positive, add a constant of +5, so that your possible score will range from +1 for very happy to +9 for very happy.

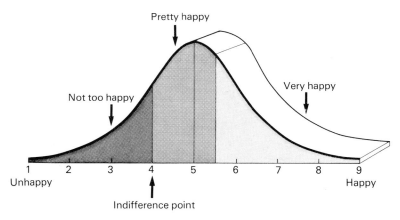

Figure 4: Drawn from a number of surveys, the figure shows the general distribution of happiness as scored by the combination of positive and negative feelings. Use your happiness-quotient score from the text on page 32 to see how happy, or unhappy, you are compared with the general population.

Figure 5 shows the normal distribution of happiness with scores from 1 to 9 at the bottom. Surprisingly enough, 30 per cent of the total population claim to be very happy, with only 15 per cent claiming unhappiness. This decidedly optimistic imbalance means that the indifference point – the point at which people are neither happy nor unhappy – is not quite at centre but roughly at +4.

A measure of happiness

Obviously one cannot measure happiness as accurately as inches and miles, and I don't pretend to do so here. But in a rough-and-ready way this little diagram does offer a reasonable measure of one's mental state, and of the way different people feel. You should be able to tell a lot about your own relative happiness, and about your position with respect to the general population.

A fix on happiness

How fleeting is happiness? If people's scores varied greatly from day to day, there would be no sense in attaching any importance to this kind of test. But, amazingly enough, repeated tests have shown a remarkable consistency in people from one occasion to another. Perhaps happiness is basically an inner state not overly affected by external conditions except in extraordinary circumstances. Obviously, if we find ourselves the victim of terrifying events, wild fluctuations will occur. These kinds of incidents, fortunately for all of us, are relatively rare in most people's lives. What is clear is that, for most people, happiness varies very little from day to day or even year to year.

Having established a broad measure of relative happiness, we can go on to look at specific factors which may affect how happy people are.

Can money buy happiness?

As Sophie Tucker once said, 'I've been poor in my life and I've been rich. Believe me, honey, rich is best.' And it is true that, at very low levels of income, where people are being crushed with heavy family responsibilities, studies show money or the lack thereof being a measure of (un)happiness. But from the very

broad range of middle-income families to the much smaller numbers of the wealthy and very wealthy, money seems to have only a marginal effect on the levels of happiness as measured in tests like Bradburn's. On the other hand, lack of money seems to have a strong effect on unhappiness.

Mental health

Mental health is very strongly related to one's happiness. Any serious mental problem that lasts over a period of time is strongly associated with an increase in negative affect. Here again it is important to remember the difference between positive feelings and negative feelings: lack of money, or long-term mental instability do not affect the things we feel happy about, but they do increase the proportion of things we feel unhappy about.

On the positive side of things

If emotional and financial problems help determine a person's negative affect score, what affects his positive range of feelings? Again, Bradburn has a possible answer in his studies: 'Social participation is associated with positive affect and not with experiences of negative affect.' Bradburn goes further to suggest that social participation divides itself into two distinct components: *sociability* and *novelty*. Fresh, new experiences play a strong part in increasing positive affect. Sociable people go out more and so increase their chances of encountering new and varied activities. In other words, if you enjoyed it once you'll want to try it again. People who experience a strong 'plus' side for positive affects are thus quite naturally going to be in a position to receive even more. It is this which makes them happy people.

Can we predict happiness?

While it is true that external factors – education, socioeconomic status, age, gender, etc. – influence one's Happiness Quotient, the surprising fact is that their effect is marginal rather than substantial. In a national survey, the American psychologist A. Campbell has reported that only 17 per cent of life satisfaction, or happiness, can be predicted from external factors. Furthermore, F. M. Andrews and S. B. Withey, in their own American sampling, found that age, income, race, and other such indicators taken either singly or in combination accounted for only 8 per cent of the total variation in happiness. Even lottery winners were judged no happier than control subjects on their own reports of estimated future happiness: there seems to be no ticket to happiness for anybody! Why is this? One psychological explanation is suggested in a concept called the '*adaptation level*'.

A standard for happiness

Based upon some studies in perception and judgment, it can be seen that our own perceptions depend upon past experiences, to which we tend to compare our present situation. We set our own standards for happiness and everything else: our level of expectation adapts itself to the level of past encounters. A poor and hungry man might be made happy by a crust of bread, whereas a rich, sated individual would find it unappetizing. To be added to 'I felt bad because I had no shoes until I met a man who had no feet' could be another person's complaint about the price of champagne. It is also interesting to note that not only do lottery winners not attain new heights in general happiness, but that the everyday pleasures they once enjoyed, such as watching television or enjoying a can of cold beer, no longer appeal!

What makes us happy?

The Bible itself states that 'He that is of a merry heart hath a continual feast.'

In other words, it is what we *imagine* ourselves to be that makes the difference. If we think we are happy, then we are. And why does one person judge himself happy and another not? Much as some people like not to think so, we are probably born that way. We are all equal under the law, but Nature herself is not quite so fair. Just as individuals differ in personality, intelligence, looks, athletic prowess, and other abilities, so do they in their potential for happiness. It may not be fair, but it's certainly true, and perhaps one of the most impressive pieces of evidence to support this idea comes from an analysis of marriage of twins to twins.

Fifty such marriages have been studied, and the results are startling as well as instructive. *In every single case the marriages had an identical outcome.* In my own study concerning the heredity factor in human happiness or unhappiness, I administered positive and negative affect scales to 386 pairs of male and female identical twins, as well as to 348 pairs of male/female

fraternal twins. The genetic factor was strikingly more obvious in the case of the identical twins, where two human beings were created from one egg, than in studies of fraternal twins who are derived from two eggs and who have no closer chromosomal relationship than ordinary brothers and sisters. While environment does play some part in one's satisfaction with life, it is clear that heredity strongly determines an individual's ability to be happy. Lenin and Marx themselves, while staunch supporters of economic egalitarianism, both mocked as an 'absurdity' the idea of extending equality into such spheres as man's mental and physical capabilities. It is sad but true that some people are simply more equal than others.

State of happiness?

How does the state of marriage affect one's state of mind? As we saw earlier, studies have shown that marital status does have some relationship to both the positive and negative affects in the measure of happiness. Divorced, separated, or widowed men and women are lower in positive affect and higher in negative affect than currently married persons, giving them a generally lower Happiness Quotient. This is true for both men and women, although *single men* do tend to be highest of all in negative affect.

Singling out the men

Why are single men unhappier than single women? One explanation has to do with our traditional marriage selection process. If men are the initiators of the marital state in our society, then perhaps maladjusted or psychically impaired men are less likely to get married in the first place, making the single male status an unhappy one by default. Studies by Dr G. Knupfer and colleagues have uncovered evidence that suggests this to be the case, and they have further shown that more psychologically impaired men than women are among the never-married. Another idea suggests that men in general react more negatively to the state of being single. They are less capable than women of establishing close relationships outside the institution of marriage, and they are generally less able to assume 'feminine' roles of housekeeping, of looking after themselves. The truth is probably somewhere in between, and it also involves a man and a woman's general attitude towards marriage in the first place.

Is a happy marriage what happiness is?

In one study Bradburn found that 56 per cent of women found their marriage 'very happy' as opposed to only 48 per cent of the men. Women were happier in their marriage than men, and women in general seemed to feel that *a happy marriage meant general happiness*. 'In fact', states Bradburn, 'the relationship for women is so strong as to suggest that most women are equating their happiness in marriage with their overall happiness.' This, of course, makes it easier for women to be happy in marriage, but it still is not a simple matter.

'Mixed' marriage

As with all other aspects of life and, specifically, concerning happiness, marital bliss is related to both the positive and negative range of feelings. Bradburn revealed this when he asked the question, 'Can marriage happiness itself be composed into two dimensions, one of positive and one of negative affect?' He went on to construct two questionnaires, one consisting of items relevant to a *marital tensions* index, the other to *marriage satisfactions*. The latter concerned itself with positive feelings and divided into two other areas, *marriage sociability* and *marriage companionship*. What Bradburn learned was that marriage like everything else in life is full of contradictions. While both questionnaires examined the state of general happiness within the marriage, there was no correlation at all between the pluses in the positive range and the added-up feelings on the negative side. In other words, a couple could spend wonderful evenings together watching television but still fight themselves into a rage over financial

Drawing by Edward Koren © 4New Yorker Magazine 1982

'*My darling, I want to share my money worries, my tensions, and my
unhappiness with you for the rest of my life.*'

disagreements. This fluctuating relationship with its many ups
and downs constitutes the 'quarrel and make up' kind of
marriage that is so often portrayed in television situation
comedies. Its counterpart, of course, where there is both a lack
of marital tension and a dearth of sociability and companionship, presents the kind of marriage where monogamy has
become monotony.

Happy to be married, or married to be happy?

Norval Glenn has moved on from the pioneering work of
Bradburn, and, in analysing the data from three recent US
national surveys, he has found that married persons report
substantially greater overall happiness than *any* category of
unmarried persons, the difference being even greater for
females than for males. There is not only a stronger relationship
between marital and overall happiness for wives; women in

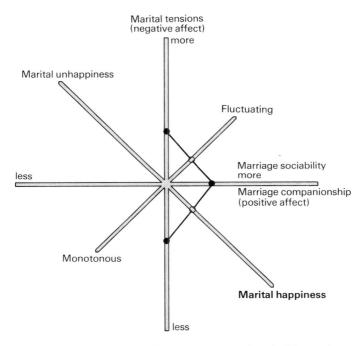

Figure 5: In marriage, positive feelings are associated with marriage sociability and companionship, negative feelings with marital tensions. Using the same method as in Figure 3, you can rate your own level of married happiness as it stands at the moment. Remember, the positive and negative axes are independent of each other: you may feel, for example, that your marriage is both high in sociability *and* in tensions. Just choose a point on both axes which you feel roughly reflects your feelings. Now join up the points to see if your marriage is more, or less, happy, *or* whether it lies on a point between equanimity and extreme ups-and-downs.

general exceed men in both the stress and satisfaction they receive in marriage. In general, however, levels of reported marital happiness are similar for husbands and wives.

Marriage as a metaphor for happiness

What is the meaning behind this close relationship between marriage and general happiness? Is marital satisfaction simply a reflection of overall happiness, or does marriage actually contribute something to one's general emotional state? Does marriage mean the same thing to all groups of people? Answers to these questions were sought by Glenn and Weaver, two American sociologists who analysed data from six US National Surveys. Over six successive years the following questions were asked of a representative sampling of the American population:

1   Taken altogether, how would you say things are these days – would you say that you are very happy, pretty happy, or not too happy?

2   Taking things altogether, how would you describe your marriage? Would you say that your marriage is very happy, pretty happy, or not too happy?

3   On the whole, how satisfied are you with the work you do – would you say you are very satisfied, moderately satisfied, a little dissatisfied, or very dissatisfied?

4   We are interested in how people are getting along financially these days. So far as you and your family are concerned, would you say that you are pretty well satisfied with your present financial situation, more or less satisfied, or not satisfied at all?

5   For each area of life I am going to name, tell me the number that shows how much *satisfaction* you get from that area: (1) a very great deal; (2) a great deal; (3) quite a lot; (4) a fair amount; (5) some; (6) a little; (7) none:

(a) Your non-working activities, hobbies and so on

(b) Your family life

(c) Your friendships

(d) Your health and physical condition

Complex statistical analyses were carried out on all the data gathered from more than 10 000 men and women. The major finding? Marital happiness was found to have a stronger relationship with overall happiness than did any other dimension of well-being. This was true of white men and women as well as black women; only black men working full time failed to have marital happiness outrank work satisfaction as a positive predictor of overall happiness. This exception undoubtedly has to do with larger socioeconomic, racial and historic issues, but the basic point is still there: namely, that for most adults happiness depends upon having a good marriage more than upon anything else.

Marriage is alive and well in the divorce courts

Glenn and Weaver have taken this basic hypothesis a step further when they look upon divorce as a search for happiness. 'Everything else being equal', they argue, 'the divorce rate will vary positively with the extent to which marriage is depended upon for personal happiness.' Because of marriage's importance to one's overall happiness, a poor marriage can itself mean unhappiness. Divorce can be looked upon then not only as a step towards happiness; its very existence predicts the continuation, the acceptance of marriage as an institution!

Children and happiness

Children form a special issue in the consideration of marriage, particularly in this divorce-ridden age when many people enter their married lives with children already part of the picture. Despite the old saw that children cement a marriage, the truth is that there is concrete evidence that their presence can impair the happiness of a marriage. Children more often than not have a negative affect on a marriage and, women's liberation to the contrary, couples with sons are less prone to divorce than those who have only daughters in their family! Here, once again, life proves itself unfair, for it is the genes that decide what sex your children will be. Fortunately, many other aspects of a marriage involve some sort of choice, and it is your own control over these that will help you take charge of at least part of your own happiness.

Computer dating

One phenomenon of the second half of the twentieth century which appears to be enjoying considerable success is computer dating. The interesting thing about the organizations who turn to technology when chance doesn't seem to be doing its stuff is that they operate on the basis of like-attracts-like – not for any proven scientific reason, but because that is what the vast majority of their customers want.

According to the people who run Dateline, Britain's biggest computer dating agency, Miss Dateline, the female most males using the system would like to meet, bears an uncanny resemblance to Mr Dateline. *She* is looking for a man who is single or divorced, who comes from Central or Northern Europe – though she wouldn't mind a Latin – is not less than five feet six, though more than five nine is preferable, and who, if possible, doesn't smoke. *He* wants a single girl, preferably from Northern or Central Europe, doesn't consider five foot six too tall, provided she isn't fat, and would rather she was a moderate drinker.

Sometimes, in fact, the Dateline computer excels itself and pairs off couples who are too close for comfort. One young woman wrote a fulsome letter to the staff when she received details of her ideal beau:

'Just for your records I thought you might be interested to know that on only my third run your computer managed to match me to an exceptional young man. He's handsome, intelligent, kind. We have exactly the same taste in music, politics, humour, hobbies . . . *everything*. We could talk endlessly about psychology, science, our backgrounds etc. He's perfect! There's only one snag – he's my brother! But I have great faith in your computer now.'

Do computer dates lead to marriage? They certainly do in the experience of Dateline, who, with 51000 men and women in their books, claim their bulging letters files point to 1000 marriages a year. Whether those marriages have an above-average chance of survival is a question Dateline say they are not yet qualified to answer.

Computer comrades

While many people in the West may scoff at the claims · made by computer dating agencies, their ideas have borne fruit in that most unfrivolous of homelands, Mother Russia.

Well aware that men, especially, are not happy in the single state, and therefore make unproductive workers, and that divorcees are one of the most unhappy groups in society, the Soviet Academy of Sciences has recommended that computer dating services should be set up on the Western model.

Now the system has been given the green light. Moreover, marriage bureaux are to be established in every Russian city – with the object of persuading couples to stay together (in Russia, a major motive for getting married is to secure a larger apartment). Meanwhile, trade union officials have been urged to encourage their single members to meet up with their peers at newly set up singles-only holiday camps!

3

Who marries whom?

If a good marriage is such an important factor in our personal happiness, why do almost half of all marriages today end in divorce, and why are so many intact marriages unhappy? Could it be that people are hampering their chances of success by selecting the wrong partner to begin with? I think there is a strong possibility that this is the case, and I'd like now to take a closer look at who marries whom, and which pairings are the most successful.

Before beginning my discussion of who marries whom, there are a few technical terms which I'd like to explain. These terms are a shorthand way of coming to grips with the vast amount of information available about the way people choose their marriage partners. If people married at random, without taking into account the other person's attractiveness, intelligence, socioeconomic status or personality relative to their own, we would have a state of *panmixia*, which simply refers to chaotic pairing in which everything is mixed up. When we find systematic departure from such random pairing, we call this *assortative mating*, meaning that people are selecting their prospective partners on the basis of one or more of the criteria mentioned above. When someone marries another who is like himself or herself, then we have *homogamy*. When a person marries someone unlike himself, we would have *heterogamy*, which is a term I've coined.

How assortative mating works
Homogamy is easy to spot when it comes to certain characteristics. For example, married couples are usually close in age. In the Western world the age difference between

'No question about it, Louise—we've been married too long.'

partners is about three years, and the man is most often the older of the two. This has been the case for most of this century, although in previous centuries older men often married much younger wives, partly because they were not able to support a family sooner, and partly because women often died in childbirth and the older man wanted to replace his wife with another woman of child-bearing age. Often, after the death of the older husband, the widow would marry a younger man. During the Victorian period these practices began to die out and they have now been replaced by the recent trend towards homogamy in terms of age.

Assortative mating is also affected by previous marital status. Someone who has never been married tends to marry someone who has also never been married, whereas divorced people tend to marry other divorced people. This tendency may be because of a similarity in age, but I suspect that psychological factors weigh more heavily.

Religion plays a big part in assortative mating. Some religions forbid believers to marry outside of the faith and almost all religions frown on such marriages. Even though the influence of many religions is weakening, people still tend to marry someone of their own faith. This is partly because people often marry someone from their own neighbourhood, and the chances are that people from the same neighbourhood will be of the same faith.

Neighbourhood determines homogamy because you can only marry someone you know. Since you know the people in your neighbourhood, the people you grew up with, went to school with, socialized with, you tend to marry someone from this group. Studies show that the birthplaces of spouses are usually close together. In a third of American surveys, for example, the place where a couple married was only ten miles from where the partners had been born, a surprisingly high proportion considering the vastness of the country, and the mobility of Americans in general.

People also tend to marry others from the same social and economic background. Again, neighbourhood plays a significant part in this selection, since most residential areas are made up of people of roughly the same social and economic status. Ethnic background, too, is an important factor in assortative mating. It has been shown that, in the United States, Irish Catholics, Italians and Poles tend to marry people within their own group. Although this tendency has been decreasing somewhat in recent years, it is still quite prevalent.

When ethnic differences are strong enough to be called racial, involving the highly visible nature of some characteristics such as skin colour or facial features, assortative mating tendencies are very strong. It is a moot point whether intermarriage between races is largely avoided because of obvious physical differences, or significant cultural differences. Intermarriage is a sensitive subject and, because of this, little research has been done on it. So, in the United States no records are being kept of the ethnic or racial origin of people who marry. In Hawaii, where there are many different races, such records are kept, and they show that the majority of marriages have been within the same ethnic group rather than between groups.

The degree of homogamy for physical traits such as eye colour, hair colour and height is not very pronounced. When it does occur, it seems to be slightly stronger for hair colour than for height, and about the same for eye colour and height, even though height is so much more obvious a trait than eye colour. Of course, it is possible that observed homogamy is indirect. In other words, perhaps it's not that tall people look for other tall people to marry, or that blonds look for blondes, but rather that people from the same social, economic and ethnic origin tend to marry each other and often the height, hair colour and eye colour within their group is similar.

Psychological factors: intelligence

What psychological traits do we look for in our partners? There are two important areas: intelligence and personality. We'll begin with intelligence. The concept of intelligence, and its measurement, are so often misunderstood that it may be as well to make it clear what we are talking about.

Psychologists make a clear distinction between intelligence – which describes a person's ability to acquire knowledge – and the amount of knowledge he or she has actually acquired. We don't usually measure intelligence by testing scholastic achievement. Rather, we tend to measure someone's cognitive ability by tests which have little relevance to what a person may have been taught. The following would be a reasonable question in an intelligence test:

2 5 9 14 20 ?

provided that everyone given the test could count to a hundred, and knew how to add and subtract. This next question, however, would not be reasonable:

La Bohème is to *Aida* as Puccini is
to which of the following:

Wagner, Verdi, Mozart, Bizet

It is impossible to create intelligence tests which are completely free from educational and cultural influences, but we can construct culture-fair tests which give us reasonably unbiased results. There is a fair amount of evidence which suggests that intelligence correlates highly with educational achievement, the kind of a job a person is able to do, and his ultimate social and economic status. It appears that differences in intelligence are strongly innate, and that they show up at an early age. In a recent study carried out on the Isle of Wight, on a group of English schoolchildren, all of whom went to a state school, an IQ test, given at the age of five (before these children had started school) forecast with very high accuracy their IQ scores at the age of 16, as well as their overall academic achievement at the school. Studies done in other countries corroborate these findings and underscore the likelihood of intelligence being largely determined by heredity, and manifesting itself early in a child's life.

When it comes to professional success, it has been found that, even within the same family, children with relatively high IQs are upwardly mobile in their careers, while their brothers and sisters with less high IQs tend to be downwardly mobile. This is in spite of the fact that these children had the same, or very similar, educations, and grew up in the same family.

There are two more points I'd like to make on intelligence. The first is that there is absolutely no difference between men and women when it comes to intelligence. The second is that intelligence is certainly not the only indicator of one's potential for high achievement. Many other measurable attributes, such as verbal agility, numerical ability, and visuo-spatial ability, go to determine the profession a person will choose, and how successful in it he or she is apt to be. There are some differences between men and women when it comes to these abilities – women tend to be better at verbal skills while men tend to excel in visuo-spatial ability. However, these differences are small, and there is a great deal of overlap.

A match for each other

The evidence is overwhelming that there is strong homogamy for general intelligence (as measured by IQ tests); in other words, intelligent men usually marry intelligent women, average men usually marry average women, and less intelligent men usually marry less intelligent women. Certainly there are exceptions to this selective mating based on intelligence, but, for the most part, homogamy rules.

In addition to general intelligence, we also find homogamy for verbal, spatial, memory and other special abilities. So, when it comes to abilities, there is overwhelming evidence that 'like marries like'.

But, how does this selection process work? One possibility is that newly marrieds may not be all that similar, but over the course of their marriage they begin to 'grow together'. In this case the brighter of the two spouses may consciously or unconsciously help the other to acquire a better vocabulary, to learn more about art and politics, to read more, and to think

more about what is happening around him. When this happens we may find marked changes in the less bright spouse's IQ test scores. Now this may seem to contradict my statement about IQ differences being largely determined by genetic factors. But there is actually no contradiction. As I have said, marriage is a biosocial institution. Genetic factors are important but they do not account for *all* observed differences in intelligence. Environmental and educational factors do play a part, in some cases a large part.

Although some couples do 'grow together', is doesn't happen as often as you might expect. If it did, then the degree of homogamy should be greater for couples who have been married for a long time than it is for the more newly wed. This does not appear to be the case. Most of the couples we have studied resemble each other from the start, and rarely does the degree of homogamy increase with advancing age.

Why, then, does this homogamy usually exist from the outset? Do men and women consciously seek a mate of the same intelligence level? I think not. It seems more likely to me that men and women meet other men and women who are somewhat like them. They meet at school, at work, at church or synagogue, at resorts or clubs – and the people they find in these places are usually from the same or similar background and quite often they are of similar intelligence. So that homogamy for intelligence happens by circumstance rather than by design.

It is clear, then, that homogamy exists as far as intelligence is concerned. But does similarity in intelligence make for a happier marriage? Apparently the answer is yes. Louis M. Terman, an American psychologist from Stanford University who carried out the first large-scale study on marital happiness, published in 1938, came to the following conclusion: 'As to relative mental ability, the most favourable situation is equality or near equality. Marked mental superiority of husband makes for happiness in the wife, but for unhappiness in the husband: marked inferiority of the husband makes the wife unhappy, but does not greatly affect the husband.' So, we are apparently unhappy if our spouses are much less intelligent than we are: if they are much brighter, it doesn't seem to bother us much, but, of course, it would probably bother our spouse, so that's where the unhappiness sets in.

Psychological factors: personality

Now let's look at personality. Fortunately the ways in which the layman and the psychologist think about personality are similar so we won't have to define terms. Psychologists talk about traits like sociability, persistence, honesty, dominance, self-sufficiency in much the same way as the man in the street. When it comes to these traits we seem to have a variety of continua, at one end of which we have people who are very self-sufficient, or very sociable, while at the other end we have people who are either very dependent on others, or who are very unsociable. Most of us lie somewhere in between.

Measuring personality traits

Personality traits can be measured in a variety of ways. The most obvious is simply to observe a person's behaviour and rate it. We can watch people in a social situation, for example, and then rate their sociability – do they seek other people's company, do they initiate conversation, do they appear relaxed and friendly when someone initiates a conversation with them? Ratings are somewhat subjective, however, and it is always a good idea to have someone rated by more than one observer.

Questionnaires are another popular way of measuring personality. The social scientist simply constructs a series of questions relating to the particular trait he is trying to measure. Then he asks his subjects to answer the questions and analyses the results. If the questionnaire is carefully constructed, the answers a person gives to the questions can tell us a lot about personality. You can find three examples of what I mean in the next chapter.

The third way of measuring personality is by creating what

we call 'miniature situations'. So, if we want to measure a man's persistence, for example, in addition to getting ratings from people who know him, and asking him to answer a questionnaire, we can put him in a situation where he can actually demonstrate his persistence. We might ask him to hold his hands out in front of him and see how long it takes before he gives up and drops them. Or, we might ask him to work on an insoluble intellectual problem and see how long he sticks with it. When we give someone this kind of test we have to watch for two things. First, is a person who is persistent in one test also persistent in others? If not, then the tests are not measuring the same thing. Second, we must ask ourselves if we are really measuring persistence or something else. Perhaps intelligent people stick with these tasks longer than others, or, perhaps intelligent people are less persistent because the test seems silly to them. By giving the person an intelligence test we can find out whether persistence is positively or negatively affected by intelligence. Once we have resolved this we can then see whether the person's persistence correlates with other people's ratings of it, and whether it is the same as the person said it was in answering the questionnaire. In other words we can end up with a pretty accurate picture of just how persistent a person is and, if we choose to, we can find out whether or not persistence has anything to do with his intelligence.

Personality and homogamy

Now that we know that we can can measure personality traits we can ask ourselves whether or not homogamy exists when it comes to personality, as it does, for example, with respect to intelligence. In general, the answer seems to be no, or at least, not very much. One way of demonstrating this is by explaining a term statisticians use. The term is 'correlation coefficient', and it is used to describe the amount of similarity between two sets of data. So, if you want to measure the personality scores of married couples, you would set up a scale which ranges from zero (which indicates no agreement at all) to 1.00 (which indicates perfect agreement). On such a scale, homogamy for intelligence is indicated by a coefficient of .50, homogamy for age by a coefficient of .76, homogamy for religion by a coefficient of .77, and homogamy for physical traits by a much lower coefficient: .30 for heighttt, .34 for hair colour, and .26 for eye colour.

The correlation for physical traits is low, but the correlation for personality traits is even lower. Take self-sufficiency, for example. Four different studies show correlations of .12, .09, .07, and .00. There is not much difference between these correlations and panmixia, or completely random selection. There is a wide variety of homogamy when it comes to dominance, too. It varies from a mild degree of homogamy to actual inverse relationships in which one partner is extremely dominant and the other extremely submissive.

Correlations averaging less than .20 have been found for such traits as adventurousness, sensitivity, suspiciousness, imaginativeness, shrewdness, proneness to guilt and nervousness. We can conclude, then, that most personality traits show either very little homogamy, or none at all.

Personality types

Most people would recognize that there are different types of personality, and that types are made up of a number of traits with something of a family likeness. Do similar personality types marry? It is possible that although traits themselves do not show much relationship between the spouses, types may be rather more similar. Psychologists divide personality types into various categories. A person may be an *extravert*; eager for new experience, active, optimistic. Another may be an *introvert*, with a tendency to being withdrawn, passive, anxious and pessimistic. Of course there are many variations. However, as far as extraversion – introversion is concerned, the evidence is against similar types marrying. There *is* a positive correlation overall, but it averages only about .10 at most – which amounts to an improvement over chance of just one per cent. This clearly is so small as to be negligible, even if not the product of other factors, like socio-ecomomic status, schooling, and so on.

Another personality type factor is variously labelled anxiety, emotional instability, or *neuroticism*. The term 'neuroticism' should be distinguished carefully from 'neurosis'. Neurosis denotes an emotional instability so great that it requires special psychiatric treatment; it is a relatively frequent reason for consulting physicians, and some one person in six at some stage of life is likely to do so. Neuroticism, on the other hand, is a term applied to perfectly normal people who are likely to range from emotionally quite stable to emotionally very unstable, with less stable individuals more likely to succumb to neurotic disorders than the most stable.

As far as neuroticism is concerned, correlations between spouses seem to be somewhat higher, although seldom exceeding .20, or at most .30; in other words, those who are unstable seem to marry others who are also unstable. But remember that a correlation of .20 only means that the likelihood of this happening is four per cent better than chance! Nevertheless, correlations for emotional instability are more frequently positive than they are for other personality traits or type concepts.

Homogamy and mental illness

This tendency might be expected to be stronger when we are dealing with people who are actually under psychiatric care at some stage of their lives. Here it may be useful to discriminate between neurosis and psychosis: the neurotic type of disorder includes feelings of anxiety, exaggerated depression on experiencing some personal loss or disappointment, obsessions and compulsions, phobic fears of spiders, or other small animals, heights, aeroplanes, darkness, open or closed spaces and other types of irrational fears which neurotics themselves usually know are groundless. Contrasted with this type of disorder are the so-called psychotic illnesses, particularly schizophrenia and manic-depressive psychosis; in these the patient is much more seriously disordered, is irrational, does not recognize the absurdity of his or her own beliefs and is usually treated with drugs rather than with some form of psychotherapy.

To take but one example, someone married to a schizophrenic is twice as likely to be diagnosed as schizophrenic than the population. In another study, Dr J. Nielsen studied the entire population of the Danish island of Samso and found that both spouses received psychiatric care in a much larger number of cases than would be expected on the basis of random mating. He, like other investigators, agreed that spouses do not become more alike as the marriage continues. From the outset of marriage both are likely to share about the same chance of developing a mental disorder. Other research has shown that psychotic seems to attract psychotic, neurotic seems to attract neurotic. Why this should be so is not known; it could be that those who are psychiatrically ill are not in a good position to ask in marriage more stable, more normal, and hence perhaps also more successful people.

One study shows that there is homogamy for some degrees of psychiatric abnormality even when the abnormality is discovered at a very early age. This, then, supports the view that homogamy does not arise because of being married to a particular type of person, but that it exists from the beginning of a marriage.

Social attitudes and values are related to personality, too, and we would expect to find more homogamy here than we have found for personality. We will discuss how we measure these values in the next chapter, but let me say here that the homogamy for personal values is about as high as it is for intelligence.

'Why did I ever marry below my emotional level!'

Homogamy for the remarried

There is a difference in homogamy between first and subsequent marriages. First marriages are more homogamous in terms of age, education and religious identification than are second marriages. In other words, divorced people tend to go further afield in looking for a second partner and they often marry someone less like themselves than they did the first time.

When you compare the degree of homogamy in current first marriages with homogamy for remarried women, the degree of homogamy in the first marriage of the remarried women is lower than it is for those women who are still married. This may mean that homogamous marriages are happier and less likely to end in divorce. We will look at this question again in the next chapter.

Homogamy for beauty

Finally, let's take a look at the ticklish issue of attractiveness. Although beauty may be only skin deep, apparently that skin counts for a great deal. Physical attractiveness plays a large part in our marital choices and it often blinds the other person to other traits which may not be attractive or compatible at all. Although there are those who deny that there is any overall agreement on what makes up physical attractiveness, the evidence contradicts them. Usually when men are asked to judge physical attractiveness in women, or when women are asked to judge physical attractiveness in men, they are in agreement. Of course, there is some disparity in all this, but not as much as you might think.

Apparently, though, we are not very accurate in our perceptions about our own attractiveness. When you ask people to state their own level of attractiveness and compare their evaluation with that of objective judges, the correlations are not high, averaging around .30. Errors are probably based on modesty, conceit and general ignorance of what is attractive to the opposite sex. It is interesting, though, that there is a sorting out which suggests that conscious self-judgments are probably not as accurate as unconscious ones when it comes to sexual choice. In other words, attractive people tend to select other attractive people, even though they may not actually think of it in that way.

But, do these attractive people tend to marry each other? In one study, students observed courting couples and rated their attractiveness on a five-point scale, with the male students rating the women, and the female students rating the men. They found a high degree of similarity between the dating partners. In fact, 85 per cent of the couples were found not to be separated by more than one scale point out of five. The more similar the couple in physical attractiveness, the happier they

seemed to be, the more affectionate and physically demonstrative they were.

In another study, researchers took wedding photographs and cut them apart, separating the original partners. Judges then rated the photographs and found that, in fact, there was a high correspondence between the attractiveness of the spouses, indicating that people do choose spouses who are on a similar level of attractiveness. This also underscores how important the subconscious is in making mate selection because, no matter how these people rated their own attractiveness on the conscious level, they actually married people on roughly the same level.

However, these positive findings only account for a certain part of all the factors involved in selecting a mate. When men were asked to rate what they wanted most in women they put attractiveness first, sexuality second and affection third. Much less important were social grace, domestic talent, understanding, moral compatibility and creativity. So, most important to men is attractiveness, which seems to carry with it the supposition that the woman is a good lover.

Women, on the other hand, put achievement first. Following achievement come leadership, money, sociability, intelligence, athletic ability and reasoning ability. They simply do not mention attractiveness or sexuality.

Who marries whom?

Forget about the tall dark handsome stranger teenage girls believe will one day sweep them up the aisle. Women do not pick their future mates for their bright eyes and good looks. Far more important to them is that they can talk comfortably to each other, feel loyalty for each other and share a good joke. A survey carried out for *Woman* magazine in 1978 by Opinion Research Centre asked 836 women a wide range of questions about their husbands and their marriages and discovered that only 2 per cent thought it important to have a handsome husband. On the other hand, 79 per cent thought being able to talk to each other was an important ingredient in a good marriage. The younger wives – 86 per cent of them – rated good communication most highly, while older wives placed greater emphasis on kindness and humour. Perhaps, it has been suggested, older couples find the best way to survive years of minor catastrophes is to learn to laugh at them.

Less than half the women believed that a good sex life was important. Moreover, even, sexual fidelity came well down the list with only a third of wives attributing major importance to it.

Courting success
The survey also revealed that it pays to know your man before you get hitched, bearing out the old adage 'marry in haste, repent at leisure'. Out of the women who said they wouldn't marry the same man again, 12 per cent had had a courtship of six months or less, a further 16 per cent between six months and a year.

This means that nearly three in ten of the wives who aren't happy in their marriages hadn't known their husbands for long before they took the plunge.

On the other hand, only 6 per cent of the women who said they would choose the same man again had a courtship of six months or less, and only 11 per cent had known their man between six months and a year.

Satisfaction in marriage

Asked how they thought their marriage had turned out, the women revealed themselves remarkably satisfied, with a third reporting that the married state had turned out better than they expected. Only 10 per cent said it had turned out less well than they expected, though this did not necessarily mean they would not choose the same man again. A higher number of young wives – 14 per cent – stated that marriage had not lived up to their starry-eyed dreams. Wives of professional men took a rosier view of how their partnership had turned out – 39 per cent said 'better than expected', while for wives of manual workers the figure was 22 per cent.

The perfect husband?

In fact the same wives, asked to rate their husbands on a 'perfection' scale, with a perfect man getting full marks, an average husband five and a no-hoper nought, gave glowing testimonies: some three-quarters of them rated their husbands above average. Nearly one in seven said their man was perfect, more than one in ten gave him a score of nine out of ten and a further one in four gave him a score of eight.

Most admiring was the 40–49 age group, where one

woman in five said she had a perfect husband. Most critical were the young wives. More of the under 25s rate their husbands average or below average than any of the other age groups. And the higher up the social scale the couple the more likely is the man to score above average marks. Predictably, the wives who say they would marry the same man again are far more likely to rate their husbands highly than those who would make a different choice given the opportunity. More intriguingly, 3 per cent of the unhappy wives rated their husband as perfect, and 40 per cent gave him an above average score, which suggests that there are factors other than the personality of the spouse affecting how people feel about marriage.

(From a survey conducted by Opinion Research Centre for *Woman* magazine, 1978)

The overall picture

With this evidence in mind, we can answer the question of who marries whom with some degree of accuracy. Married partners tend to be alike when it comes to age, ethnic background and religion. They also are from similar socioeconomic backgrounds (which increases the likelihood that they will have had a similar education). They share attitudes and values, and are similar in intelligence and sociability. And, as we've just discussed, they are similar when it comes to physical attractiveness. In all these factors, then, there is homogamy or positive assortative mating going on. When it comes to these qualities, it's true that like marries like.

But, when it comes to personality, there is very little evidence of homogamy, except to a very slight and socially insignificant extent. Extraverted people do not marry extraverted people any more than introverted people marry introverts. It is almost impossible to predict a person's choice of a marriage partner on the basis of his or her personality. The only slight exception to this is in the area of emotional instability, where we find a small tendency for homogamy. The greater the psychiatric disability the greater this tendency appears to be. But, even in people attending a psychiatrist, the degree of homogamy is still lower than it is, for instance, with respect to intelligence. So, as far as normal personality is concerned, there is almost complete panmixia.

This is a very important finding because it may mean that a more careful selection of your mate, based on his or her having personality traits similar to yours, may be a strong indicator of a happy marriage. If this is true it could save a lot of heartache and anguish, not to mention legal fees. If, too, we can learn to recognize our own personality traits and spot them in others, we may be on the way to having some hard and fast information that will help us to have the loving and fulfilling marriage we all crave. I will look into this more closely in the next chapter.

4

Personality and satisfaction in marriage

Homogamous/monogamous

As we have seen, similarity, or homogamy, tends to prevail in most marriages. People who like the same things tend to get married; people who *are* alike in many ways – social class, intelligence, educational background, etc. – also more often form legal attachments. However, like marrying like does *not* mean that the partners necessarily like their union. Like it or not, the question of who is happy in marriage is entirely divorced, often quite literally, from who marries whom. Happiness is really more a question of personality, not simply the fit between two partners in a marriage, but the personality that *you* carry with you wherever you go, both in and out of the marital state.

Vive la différence?

Two opposing theories on the secret of marital satisfaction have been around about as long as the battle between the sexes itself. One camp expounds upon the importance of *similarity*. According to this theory, you simply get on better with someone who is like you: sociable males should marry sociable females; extraverted males should reach out for extraverted females, and so on. Then there is the law of *complementarity*. A man and a woman should not only compliment but complement one another. Plato wrote about this theory some 2 500 years ago, and many people still believe that the answer for a dominant male is a submissive female, for a sociable woman a misanthropic man, and so on. However, the truth about the

'It's our <u>own</u> story <u>exactly</u>! He bold as a hawk, she soft as the dawn.'

question of personality is far less simple than either of these theories.

A show of temperament

We have already seen the complexities involved in measuring a person's happiness; personality is an equally complicated matter. There are two major directional factors operating in personality, the issue of extraversion versus introversion and the feature of emotional stability versus instability and/or neuroticism. But even these form a long-ranging continuum rather than a simple distinction.

The ancient Greeks divided human temperaments into four types: Melancholic, Choleric, Sanguine, and Phlegmatic. We still use these terms today in their almost literal derivation but the notion of four distinct and separate temperaments is far from accurate. The truth is a continuum, a blending of types, and the intermediate stage of 'ambiversion' more accurately describes most people than a simple branding of extravert versus introvert. But the diagrammatic form of Figure 6 clearly shows a definite relation of qualities within the four given types, so that people who can be called emotionally unstable introverts are recognizably 'melancholic'; likewise, an aggressive, optimistic person fits in with the general 'choleric' description.

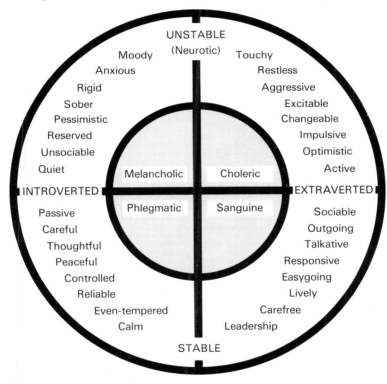

Figure 6: Two major 'type' concepts of human personality: extraversion–introversion, and emotional stability versus instability (or neuroticism). The qualities, or traits, ranged round the circle give an idea of the characteristics which go to make up each type of personality. Inside the circle you can see how the ancient Greeks divided human temperaments into four main types. Even today we still speak of someone as being of a 'melancholic' or a 'sanguing' disposition. The diagram relates both ancient and modern methods of identifying personality types.

Personality types
Most people tend to have the majority of their personality
qualities in the same quadrant. Most neurotics, for instance,
whether specifically depressed or anxious, tend to be introverted and unstable – in other words, melancholic. You meet
more criminals in the unstable, extraverted or choleric
quadrant, and if you actually *have* met a lot of criminals, you're
probably an active extravert yourself. These are admittedly
rough-and-ready descriptions, but it is still true that you tend
to meet more sanguine paratroopers than melancholic ones;
and it certainly aids a scientist's career to be a phlegmatic,
stable introvert.

A personality for happiness
There is no question that one's personality is related to one's
chances for happiness; quite *how* is more difficult to judge. For
there really is no easy solution; once again, there seems to be a
continuum operating within the human psyche, some aspects
of one's personality contributing to one's happiness, other
qualities actually detracting from it. And which does which can
be very surprising! The questionnaires in this chapter will help

you understand the traits that make up your own personality. The first group of questions relates to the introversion/extraversion aspect of your personality; the second deals with your stability – or instability, if that happens to be the case. In each questionnaire a person who is exactly intermediate between the two extremes would get a score of 25; higher scores than 25 indicate a greater degree of extraversion and instability on the two tests, lower, introversion and stability. Of course, the more you deviate from the average score of 20–30, the more extreme your personality or temperament is as regards extraversion, introversion, stability, and instability.

Extraversion–Introversion Scale

1. Do you like going out a lot? Yes ? No

2. Are you happiest when you get involved in some project that calls for rapid action? Yes ? No

3. Would you rather read the sports page than the editorial leaders in a newspaper? Yes ? No

4. If you are watching a slapstick film or farcical play do you laugh louder than most of the people around you? Yes ? No

5. Are you inclined to live each day as it comes along? Yes ? No

6. Generally, do you prefer reading to meeting people? Yes ? No

7. Are you frequently lacking in energy and motivation to do things? Yes ? No

8. Do you like to have time to be alone with your thoughts? Yes ? No

9. Do you sit calmly when you are watching a race or competitive sport? Yes ? No

10. Are you inclined to be overconscientious? Yes ? No

75

11. Are you fairly talkative when you are with a group of people?　　　Yes ? No

12. Do you become restless when working at something in which there is little action?　　　Yes ? No

13. Do you seldom stop to analyse your own thoughts and feelings?　　　Yes ? No

14. Is your anger quick and short?　　　Yes ? No

15. Do you often leave things to the last minute?　　　Yes ? No

16. Do you hate being with a crowd who play practical jokes on one another?　　　Yes ? No

17. Are you inclined to be slow and deliberate in your actions?　　　Yes ? No

18. Do you frequently pause just to meditate about things in general?　　　Yes ? No

19. Would you refrain from expressing your attitudes and opinions if you thought that others present might be offended by them?　　　Yes ? No

20. Are you normally on time for appointments?　　　Yes ? No

21. Do you like talking to people so much that you never miss a chance of talking to a stranger?　　　Yes ? No

22. Do you usually finish your meals faster than other people even though there is no reason to hurry?　　　Yes ? No

23. Would you rather see a comedy than a documentary on TV?　　　Yes ? No

24. Are you so carried away by music that you are usually compelled to conduct or dance in time with it?　　　Yes ? No

25. Do you have a tendency to 'let things slide' occasionally?　　　Yes ? No

26. If you were making a business enquiry would you rather write than discuss it on the telephone?   Yes ? No

27. Do you prefer holidays that are quiet and restful without a great deal of rushing about?   Yes ? No

28. Do you like to solve 'brain teasers'?   Yes ? No

29. When you are angry with someone do you wait until you have cooled off before tackling them about the incident?   Yes ? No

30. Do you live by the maxim that a job worth doing is worth doing well?   Yes ? No

31. Are you relaxed and self-confident in the company of other people?   Yes ? No

32. Are you generally very enthusiastic about starting a new project or undertaking?   Yes ? No

33. Do you like work that involves action rather than profound thought and study?   Yes ? No

34. Do you subscribe to the philosophy of 'Eat, drink, and be merry, for tomorrow we die'?   Yes ? No

35. Are you ordinarily a carefree person?   Yes ? No

36. Do you enjoy spending long periods of time by yourself?   Yes ? No

37. Most days, are there times when you enjoy just sitting and doing nothing?   Yes ? No

38. Do you often spend an evening just reading a book?   Yes ? No

39. Can you keep an exciting secret for a long period of time?   Yes ? No

40. Would you say that generally you have a serious and responsible attitude toward the world?   Yes ? No

41. **Do you like mixing with lots of other people?**   Yes ? No

42. **When you are walking with other people do they often have difficulty keeping up with you?**   Yes ? No

43. **Are you bored with museums that feature archaeology and classical history?**   Yes ? No

44. **Are you forever buying silly little gifts for people even though there is no occasion that calls for it?**   Yes ? No

45. **Are you generally unconcerned about the future?**   Yes ? No

46. **Are you more distant and reserved than most people?**   Yes ? No

47. **Would you rather watch sports than play them?**   Yes ? No

48. **Are you so thoughtful and reflective that your friends sometimes call you a dreamer?**   Yes ? No

49. **Would you find it impossible to make a speech 'off the cuff'?**   Yes ? No

50. **Would you go out of your way to find a rubbish bin rather than throw a wrapper on the street?**   Yes ? No

Key to Extroversion–Introversion Scale

Score a 'Yes' answer 1 plus point, a 'No' answer 1 minus point, and a '?' not at all on questions 1, 2, 3, 4, 5, 11, 12, 13, 14, 15, 21, 22, 23, 24, 25, 31, 32, 33, 34, 35, 41, 42, 43, 44, 45.

Score a 'Yes' answer minus 1 point, a 'No' answer plus 1 point, and a '?' not at all on questions 6, 7, 8, 9, 10, 16, 17, 18, 19, 20, 26, 27, 28, 29, 30, 36, 37, 38, 39, 40, 46, 47, 48, 49, 50.

If your score is zero, you are the ideal ambivert, i.e. neither extraverted nor introverted, but exactly in the middle. Deviations in the direction of a *positive* score suggest *extraversion*, in the direction of a *negative* score *introversion*. The greater the score, the greater the deviation.

Emotional Stability–Instability Scale

1. Do you think you are able to do things as well as most other people?   Yes ? No

2. Would you say that you seldom ever lose sleep over your worries?   Yes ? No

3. Would you walk under a ladder on the street rather than go out of your way to detour around it?   Yes ? No

4. Can you relax quite easily when sitting or lying down?   Yes ? No

5. If you have done something morally reprehensible can you quickly forget it and direct your thoughts to the future?   Yes ? No

6. Do you feel that you have little to be proud of?   Yes ? No

7. Is life often a strain for you?   Yes ? No

8. Do you blush more often than most people?   Yes ? No

9. Do you sometimes have ideas run through your head repeatedly that you would like to stop but can't?   Yes ? No

10. Do you worry unnecessarily over things that might happen?   Yes ? No

11. Are you never troubled by feelings of guilt?   Yes ? No

12. Do you often wake up sweating after having a bad dream?   Yes ? No

13. In general are you pretty sure of yourself?   Yes ? No

14. Are you usually calm and not easily upset?   Yes ? No

15. Can you easily disregard little mistakes and inaccuracies?   Yes ? No

16. Do you often get blamed or punished when you don't deserve it?   Yes   ?   No

17. Do you often think of yourself as a failure?   Yes   ?   No

18. Do you sometimes feel that you have so many difficulties that you cannot possibly overcome them?   Yes   ?   No

19. Do you often feel restless as though you want something but do not really know what?   Yes   ?   No

20. Are you never bothered by an unimportant thought that runs through your mind for days?   Yes   ?   No

21. Do you frequently feel faint?   Yes   ?   No

22. Are you easily 'rattled' if things don't go according to plan?   Yes   ?   No

23. Do you often catch yourself apologizing when you are not really at fault?   Yes   ?   No

24. Do you think that you are quite popular with people in general?   Yes   ?   No

25. Are you less prone to anxiety than most of your friends?   Yes   ?   No

26. Can you drop off to sleep quite easily at night?   Yes   ?   No

27. Do you usually feel well and strong?   Yes   ?   No

28. Is it easy for you to forget the things that you have done wrong?   Yes   ?   No

29. Are there a lot of things about yourself that you would change if you could?   Yes   ?   No

30. Are you inclined to tremble and perspire if you are faced with a difficult task ahead?   Yes   ?   No

31. Do you often worry unreasonably over things that do not really matter?   Yes   ?   No

32. Is your appetite usually good?   Yes   ?   No

33. Are you often afraid of things and people that you know would not really hurt you?   Yes ? No

34. Is there something you have done that you will regret all your life?   Yes ? No

35. Do people regard you as useful to have around?   Yes ? No

36. If you have made an awkward social error can you forget it quite easily?   Yes ? No

37. Are you normally in good health?   Yes ? No

38. Do you think it is a waste of time going to the doctor with most mild complaints such as coughs, colds and influenza?   Yes ? No

39. Do you usually feel that you can accomplish the things that you want to?   Yes ? No

40. Are you a nervous person?   Yes ? No

41. Are you easily startled by someone appearing unexpectedly?   Yes ? No

42. Do you have headaches only very rarely?   Yes ? No

43. Do you worry too long over humiliating experiences?   Yes ? No

44. Do you sometimes feel that you can never do anything right?   Yes ? No

45. Do you worry a great deal over money matters?   Yes ? No

46. Would you stay calm and collected in the face of an emergency?   Yes ? No

47. Have you ever felt you needed to take tranquillizers?   Yes ? No

48. Do you worry a lot about other members of your family getting ill?   Yes ? No

49. Do you often feel ashamed of things that you have done?   Yes ? No

81

50. Would you describe yourself as self-conscious? Yes ? No

Key to Emotional Stability–Instability Scale

Score a 'Yes' answer 1 plus point, a 'No' answer 1 minus point, and a '?' not at all on questions, 1, 2, 3, 4, 5, 6, 11, 13, 14, 15, 16, 20, 24, 25, 26, 27, 28, 32, 35, 36, 37, 38, 39, 42, 46.

Score a 'Yes' answer 1 minus point, a 'No' answer 1 plus point, and a '?' not at all on questions 7, 8, 9, 10, 12, 17, 18, 19, 21, 22, 23, 29, 30, 31, 33, 34, 40, 41, 43, 44, 45, 47, 48, 49, 50.

If your score is zero, you are just above average, i.e. neither stable nor unstable emotionally. Deviations in the direction of a *positive* score indicate stability, in the direction of a *negative* score instability. The greater the score, the greater the deviation.

Psychoticism–Superego Scale

1. If someone does you a bad turn do you feel obliged to do something about it? Yes ? No

2. Do you prefer to conceal from other people what your motives are for doing things? Yes ? No

3. Do you often buy things on impulse? Yes ? No

4. Do you think that if someone is rude to you it is best to let it pass? Yes ? No

5. Do you think that honesty is always the best policy? Yes ? No

6. Do you like planning things well ahead of time? Yes ? No

7. Would you like to watch an execution if you were given the opportunity? Yes ? No

8. Would you be more upset by losing some valuable property than hearing that a friend was seriously ill? Yes ? No

9. Do you often get into a jam because you do things without thinking? Yes ? No

10. Would you hesitate to shoot a burglar who was escaping with some of your property?   Yes ? No

11. Do you think that politicians are generally sincere and doing their best for the country?   Yes ? No

12. Before making up your mind, do you carefully consider all the advantages and disadvantages?   Yes ? No

13. Have you ever felt as though you would genuinely like to kill somebody?   Yes ? No

14. Do you think that fools deserve to be parted from their money?   Yes ? No

15. Do you usually do and say things without stopping to think?   Yes ? No

16. Do you quickly forgive people who let you down?   Yes ? No

17. Does a sense of fair play restrict your business acumen?   Yes ? No

18. When you go on a trip do you like to plan routes and timetables carefully?   Yes ? No

19. Do you dislike playing pranks on people when this might seriously annoy them?   Yes ? No

20. Are you adept in the use of white lies?   Yes ? No

21. Are you an impulsive person?   Yes ? No

22. Did you stay out of physical fights when you were a child?   Yes ? No

23. If you want someone to do something for you do you tell them your true reasons rather than offer reasons which might be more acceptable and persuasive?   Yes ? No

24. Do you usually think carefully before doing anything?   Yes ? No

25. Do you often make biting or sarcastic remarks about other people?   Yes   ?   No

26. Do you agree that it is naive and dangerous to place your complete trust in another person?   Yes   ?   No

27. Do you prefer activities that just happen to those planned in advance?   Yes   ?   No

28. Would you say that you lose your temper less often than most people?   Yes   ?   No

29. Do you feel a great deal of sympathy for the underdog?   Yes   ?   No

30. Do you prefer to 'sleep on it' before making decisions?   Yes   ?   No

31. Do you often blame other people when something goes wrong?   Yes   ?   No

32. Do you believe it is necessary to cut corners here and there in order to get on in the world?   Yes   ?   No

33. Would you agree that planning things ahead takes the fun out of life?   Yes   ?   No

34. Are you usually able to refrain from expressing your irritation?   Yes   ?   No

35. Are you drawn toward people who are sick and unfortunate?   Yes   ?   No

36. Do you frequently become so involved with a question or problem that you have to keep thinking about it until you arrive at a satisfactory solution?   Yes   ?   No

37. If somebody annoys you do you usually tell him what you think of him in no uncertain terms?   Yes   ?   No

38. Are you generally cool and detached in your dealings with other people?   Yes   ?   No

39. Do you think an evening out is more successful if it is arranged at the last moment?   Yes   ?   No

40. Would you rather say you agree with someone than start an argument?   Yes ? No

41. Do you think that most people are basically good and kind?   Yes ? No

42. Do you ever walk across the street against a red light?   Yes ? No

43. When you get into a rage do you do a lot of physical things like stamping your feet or kicking things?   Yes ? No

44. Do you occasionally have to hurt other people to get what you want?   Yes ? No

45. Can you usually manage to be patient, even with fools?   Yes ? No

46. Do some of your friends regard you as too good-natured and easily taken in?   Yes ? No

47. Do you usually take care of your own interests before worrying about those of other people?   Yes ? No

48. Do you normally tell the truth even though you might be better off lying?   Yes ? No

49. Can you easily disregard the feelings of other people in order to deal more expediently with them?   Yes ? No

50. Do you gain a lot of pleasure out of helping other people?   Yes ? No

Key to Psychoticism–Superego Scale

Score a 'Yes' answer 1 *plus* point, a 'No' answer 1 *minus* point, and a '?' not at all on questions, 1, 2, 3, 7, 8, 9, 13, 14, 15, 20, 21, 25, 26, 27, 31, 32, 33, 37, 38, 39, 42, 43, 44, 47, 49.

Score a 'Yes' answer *minus* 1 point, a 'No' answer *plus* 1 point, and a '?' not at all on questions 4, 5, 6, 10, 11, 12, 16, 17, 18, 19, 22, 23, 24, 28, 29, 30, 34, 35, 36, 40, 41, 45, 46, 48, 50.

If your score is zero, you are pretty average on this scale. *Positive* scores suggest aggressive, egocentric and impulsive personality traits, *negative* scores suggest altruistic, benevolent, tender personality traits. The higher your score, the stronger are these tendencies.

Personality scales

These three scales, of 50 items each, have been included in this book to illustrate the meaning attaching to the major personality types: extravert versus introvert, emotionally stable versus unstable, and psychotic versus altruistic. Readers may like to fill in the scales and see what their scores are, but it should be emphasized that such an exercise does not constitute scientific measurement, and should not be taken too seriously. Properly standardized questionnaires have been published, and are available to trained psychologists; these scales are intended as illustrations, and although the scores will indicate the direction of a given person's behaviour tendencies, they should not be used to diagnose your failings, but rather to give you a rough idea where you are located within the descriptive scheme of personality around which this book is structured.

Note particularly that even quite high scores on emotional instability or psychoticism do not normally indicate actual psychiatric abnormality; a high score on neuroticism may indicate an artistic temperament, a high score on psychoticism originality and creativity. If your answers lead you to the melancholic conclusion that you are not perfect, be reassured: none of us is!

No degree of perfection

There is no 'ideal' score which represents the 'ideal' combination of personality traits. No direction or degree your personality takes indicates either superiority or inferiority. An extraverted personality might make you more popular at college parties, but being an introvert is likely to get you better exam results. Introverts tend to learn better and be more reliable.

The same holds true for emotional stability versus instability. An *excess* of instability may be a bad thing, leading to neurosis and unhappiness, but a lesser degree of the same may be related to artistic ability and expressiveness. Likewise, a very stable person may have such a lack of emotion that he or she is unable to appreciate music and other artistic sources of satisfaction. It is all a matter of degree.

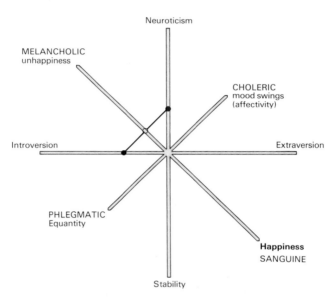

Figure 7: If you've completed the personality questionnaires you can see how your personality relates to your potential for happiness. Mark a point on the introversion–extraversion axis which roughly indicates whether you scored low, medium or high on the introversion–extraversion questionnaire. Now do the same for your score on the emotional stability–instability questionnaire: mark a point on the stability axis. Join the two points and see whether the line cuts across the happiness–unhappiness dimension or the equanimity–mood swing dimension. The point of intersection will give you a rough picture of your state of mind in relation to your personality.

Happiness is a thing called stable extraversion

It is meaningless to talk about superiority or inferiority in personality types, because people's differing values and needs make them appraise what is desirable and undesirable differently. On the other hand, happiness is a more measurable matter. There is no such thing as a 'better' personality, but the positive and negative affects of happiness discussed in earlier chapters do seem to be related to certain personality types. If you remember that the positive affect in happiness seemed to be related to easy sociability, with a natural, pleasant interaction with other people, then it only makes sense that happiness can also be associated with extraversion. Similarly, if worries and anxieties make up the negative affect in happiness, it can easily be seen that instability and neuroticism are also connected to unhappiness. Scientific investigation has demonstrated that all this is true.

Plotting your happiness

Figure 7 clearly shows the relationship between happiness and stable extraversion, and unhappiness with unstable introversion. And here again, as we could see with earlier graphs about happiness, the opposite end of positive affect is not negative affect but the *absence* of positive affect; similarly, the opposite end of negative affect is not positive affect but the *absence* of negative affect. It all makes for an interesting and complex continuum that again shows the diversity in human personality. If we look at both the positive and negative affects separately, for example, people in the choleric quadrant are likely to be extraverted and emotionally unstable and therefore capable of great mood swings, from happiness to abject misery, in very short periods of time. By the same token, the stable introvert seen in the phlegmatic quadrant would show a remarkably even mood, contented if never wildly ecstatic.

Happiness and the individual

Judging from the importance of a person's own genetically-induced personality and built-in Happiness Quotient, *the most important person you bring into your marriage is yourself.* Some people are happy regardless of the circumstances of their marriage or whom they bring into it; others will be generally unhappy under any conditions. The Greeks again had a word, or words, for it: Know Thyself. It is only if you understand who *you* are, how generally happy *you* are, how stable or unstable or introverted or extraverted *you* are, that you will be able to judge the conditions which will make you happy, and the kind or kinds of person you can happily adjust to within a prospective marriage.

Psychoticism and the superego

Psychologists have coined another term – *psychoticism* – that describes a separate dimension of the human personality, and which unfortunately has come to have melodramatic associations. It describes a personality pattern which predisposes a person to breakdowns along psychotic lines under stress, comparable to the way the made-up word 'neuroticism' serves as a synonym for emotional instability. *It does not mean that one is psychotic.* A typical behaviour pattern for a person achieving high scores in psychoticism who is not actually psychotic would make him or her emotionally cold, egotistical, aggressive, antisocial, lacking in feeling for interpersonal relations, egocentric, and generally hostile. At the opposite end of the psychoticism scale is what the Freudians describe as the 'superego' – the altruistic, emotionally responsive, friendly, helpful, and warm personality.

This matter of psychoticism, a dimension independent of extraversion/introversion and neuroticism/stability, has a high degree of difference between men and women, *males typically having higher scores than females.* Here again we have to deal with the genetic influence, for it would appear that the secretion of androgens or male sex hormones determines the high degree of psychoticism. Whether it is good or bad to be a 'High-P' scorer, however, is another matter altogether. On certain levels it makes for creative, intelligent people: at its extreme we find cold, selfish, manipulative individuals who act without remorse. As with everything else we have discussed, it is all a matter of degree.

The chance of happiness

The 50-question test for the degree of psychoticism in one's personality will again help you determine how happy you might be in marriage – in any marriage. As High-N scorers fared low in happiness, so High-P scorers tend to be relatively unhappy in marriage no matter who they married. Studies have shown, however, that there is a higher chance for happiness if it is the man who has the higher P score than the woman. So there is still an element of control in the matter of the search for a happy marriage: if you cannot control what you bring into marriage yourself, you do have some choice in what the other person brings, in the selection of your partner.

A measure of satisfaction

If you know how to understand your personality you can go on to relate it to your marital satisfaction potential. Adapting the widely used Locke-Wallis questionnaire, I created this test using fifteen of their original items and six new ones. In filling out the questionnaire, disregard the numbers written in while you are taking it, for they are only there to help you derive a score after you have completed the test. For questions 1–6 the number given in brackets indicates the number of points you score for any particular answer. For number 7, your score is the number of items ticked. There are ten sub-items for number 10, and you will see the number of points given for any particular answer for each of these sub-items. These again should be added to your total score. Finally, at the bottom of the questionnaire there is a continuum extending from unhappy – zero points – to perfectly happy, or 35 points.

You should compare your score with that of the reasonably average marriage. A score of 165 is about average, any score achieved above that meaning you are happier than most married couples, less happily married if you had a lower score.

Marital Satisfaction Inventory

All the questions in this section can be answered by placing a tick next to the appropriate answer. Please fill out all the items. If you cannot give the exact answer to a question, answer the best you can. Give the answers that best fit your marriage at the present time.

1. **Have you ever wished you had not married?**
   Frequently __ (0), occasionally __ (3), rarely __ (8).

2. **If you had your life to live over again would you:**
   Marry the same person __ (15), marry a different person __ (0), not marry at all __ (1).

3. **Do husband and wife engage in outside activities together?**
   All of them __ (10), some of them __ (8), few of them __ (3), one of them __ (0).

4. **In leisure time, which do you prefer?**
   Both husband and wife to stay at home __ (10), both to be on the go __ (3), one to be on the go and the other to stay at home __ (2).

5. **Do you and your partner generally talk things over together?**
   Never __ (0), now and then __ (2), almost always __ (10), always __ (10).

6. **How often do you kiss your partner?**
   Every day __ (10), now and then __ (5), almost never __ (2).

7. **Tick any of the following items which you think have caused *serious* difficulties in your marriage (one point per tick).**

   > **Partner's attempt to control my spending money**
   > **Other difficulties over money**
   > **Religious differences**
   > **Different amusement interests**
   > **Lack of mutual friends**
   > **Constant bickering**
   > **Interference of in-laws**
   > **Lack of mutual affection (no longer in love)**
   > **Unsatisfying sex relations**

Selfishness and lack of co-operation
Partner paid attention to (became familiar with)
    another person
Adultery
Desire to have children
Sterility of husband or wife
Venereal diseases
Desertion
Non support
Drunkenness
Gambling
Ill health
Partner in jail
Other reasons

8. When disagreements arise they generally result in:
Husband giving in ___ (0), wife giving in ___ (2), neither
giving in ___ (0), agreement by mutual give and take ___ (10).

9. What is the total number of times you left your partner or
your partner left you because of conflict?
Never ___ (10), once or more ___ (0).

State the appropriate extent of agreement or disagreement
between husband and wife on the following items:

	Always agree	Almost always agree	Occasionally disagree	Frequently disagree	Almost always disagree	Always disagree
Handling family finance	5	4	3	2	1	0
Matters of recreation	5	4	3	2	1	0
Demonstration of affection	8	6	4	2	1	0
Friends	5	4	3	2	1	0

	Always agree	Almost always agree	Occasionally disagree	Frequently disagree	Almost always disagree	Always disagree
Intimate relations (example: sex relations)	15	12	9	4	1	0
Ways of dealing with in-laws	5	4	3	2	1	0
The amount of time that should be spent together	5	4	3	2	1	0
Conventionality (example: good or proper conduct)	5	4	3	2	1	0
Aims, goals and things believed to be important in life	5	4	3	2	1	0

On the scale line below tick the mark which best describes the degree of happiness, everything considered, of your marriage. The middle point, 'happy' represents the degree of happiness which most people get from marriage, and the scale gradually ranges on one side to those few people who experience extreme joy in marriage and on the other to those who are very unhappy in marriage.

(0)		(2)	(7)	(15)	(20)	(25)	(35)
*		*	*	*	*	*	*
Unhappy				Happy			Perfectly happy

Has marriage changed?

Most of what follows is based upon research involving 566 couples married up to 40 years. Studies in earlier times and in

93

other countries are also used, however, and the end results are similar enough to suggest that not much has changed – that what was relevant to a happy marriage 50 years ago is still important, both here and elsewhere. So what have we learned?

For one thing, it would appear that there is considerable agreement between men and women on the degree of marital satisfaction that they experience. Despite some upswing in marital satisfaction among couples married for long periods of time (which may only mean that all unhappier couples found their own satisfaction in divorce earlier on . . .), there was a gradual, albeit small, overall decline in happiness in marriage over the years. Perhaps marriage is no different from anything else as we get older. As far as homogamy goes, there seemed to be little like marrying like as regards extraversion and introversion, with only a slightly higher degree of similarity in the areas of neuroticism and psychoticism. Furthermore, it is wise to remember the old adage about how you cannot change people: spouses did not tend to become more like one another as they were married as far as personality was concerned. Homogamy does not grow out of monogamy.

How do our personalities relate to marital happiness? There seems to be only a slight positive relationship between extraversion and satisfaction, and more on the part of males than females; however, there is quite a noticeable *negative* connection between neuroticism/psychoticism and marital happiness, the higher the degree, the lower the happiness.

Depletion or completion?

So far we have only looked at the personality scores of individuals – how each person's personal qualities affected his or her chances for happiness. But what about the other partner? Do we influence our spouse's chance for happiness by our own personality? As far as psychoticism goes, there is little evidence of any effect. People with similar N-scores, however, did show a higher degree of marital satisfaction, proving that in some cases misery does love company.

The asymmetry factor

In the general population, men tend to have higher psychotic-ism and lower neuroticism scores than females. Psychologists call this difference 'asymmetry' meaning 'unequally proportioned'. Should asymmetry be a goal in marriage as well as a reality in our general existence? Studies seem to indicate that the answer is yes. The differences were created for a purpose, and they may possibly be the only interaction effect between the spouses' personalities that can and *should* make a difference. Like it or not, couples are happier if the man has the higher P-score, and the woman the higher N-score. You cannot alter your own personality, but you can look carefully at that of your prospective partner, and it appears to pay if you mind your Ps and Ns. Whether this slight difference between aggression levels in men and women is socially or biologically determined is not really known and not really the point. I suspect it is a combination of both, a topic we'll deal with in a later chapter.

A negative approach

What about the reverse case? According to studies made on divorced couples, a higher P-score in women does have an effect on the stability of marriage. In one project in which some 1 500 married or divorced men and women were interviewed and questioned with the same personality-scoring tests as have been discussed thus far, the importance of the P-scoring factor became quite apparent. Female divorced informants had significantly higher P-scores than the married women; likewise for divorced men. The same was true for neuroticism, and there was a general tendency that indicated that an abnormal (in the strictly statistical sense) female personality caused more damage in a marriage than an abnormal male one. However, extraverted males tended to be more likely to get divorced than extraverted females; given that sexual promiscuity is a feature of the extraverted personality, this may be accounted for by extra-marital sexual adventures on the part of males.

Emotional incompatibility

Generally speaking, most studies indicate that the most destructive variable in marriage is and always will be *emotional instability*. We can explain this by pointing to the evidence that, the higher the neuroticism rating, the less adaptable a person is likely to be.

The critical factor of emotional stability seems to hold true no matter where the testing is done. Dr Szopinski, a Polish psychologist working with 123 married couples in Poland, found that Polish brides tended to stay married, and happily so, in cases where there was a lower degree of neuroticism and psychoticism. It would seem to be commonsense that emotionally unstable, unusually aggressive, and overly egocentric people tend to make strange, if not unpleasant and short-lived, bedfellows. Marital bliss seems to be not so much a result of what your marriage creates but what created the marriage in the first place.

Politics in the bedroom

Findings show that political beliefs and social attitudes do affect the chances of success in marriage. Two aspects are measured in the questionnaire below: a political dimension, radicalism versus conservatism (R), and an attitude dimension, which measures what we call toughmindedness and tendermindedness (T). It is easy to imagine a toughminded left-winger or a toughminded right-winger, but many people, whether of the left or the right, are more moderate. Obviously people's feelings will overlap – you may like Margaret Thatcher's foreign policy while deploring the state of the economy – but, generally speaking, one's political and social attitudes can be measured. There seems to be much evidence for homogamy on these issues, hereafter referred to as R and T, and perhaps this is just another variation on the general observation that like prefers like on issues of socioeconomics, education, residence, living habits, and so on. In general, studies show that the degree of homogamy for radicalism didn't matter as far as marital satisfaction went; however, asymmetry pops up again in the issue of tendermindedness. Couples in which the man was more toughminded seemed to have happier marriages; tendermindedness in the woman seemed to matter as well. This, of course, is somewhat dependent upon social attitudes, and that brings us to a new and more controversial point.

Social Attitudes Questionnaire

Below are given statements which represent widely-held opinions on various social questions. They were chosen in such a way that most people are likely to agree with some, and to disagree with others.

After each statement, please record your personal opinion regarding it. You should use the following system of marking:

Mark 'A' if you strongly agree with the statement
    'B' if you agree on the whole
    'C' if you can't decide for or against, or if you think the question is worded in such a way that you can't give an answer
    'D' if you disagree on the whole
    'E' if you strongly disagree.

Please answer frankly. Remember this is not a test; there are no 'right' or 'wrong' answers. The answer required is your own personal opinion. Be sure not to omit any questions. Do not consult any other person while you are giving your answers.

A, B, C, D, or E

1. **Ultimately, private property should be abolished and complete socialism introduced.** _____

2. **Production and trade should be free from government interference.** _____

3. **Divorce laws should be altered to make divorce easier.** _____

A, B, C, D, or E

4. The so-called underdog deserves little sympathy or help from successful people. _____

5. Crimes of violence should be punished by flogging. _____

6. The nationalization of the great industries is likely to lead to inefficiency, bureaucracy and stagnation. _____

7. Men and women have the right to find out whether they are sexually suited before marriage (e.g. by trial marriage). _____

8. 'My country right or wrong' is a saying which expresses a fundamentally desirable attitude. _____

9. The average man can live a good enough life without religion. _____

10. There is no survival of any kind after death. _____

11. The death penalty is barbaric, and should be abolished. _____

12. There may be a few exceptions, but in general, Jews are pretty much alike. _____

13. The dropping of the first atom bomb on a Japanese city, killing thousands of innocent women and children, was morally wrong and incompatible with our kind of civilization. _____

14. Birth control, except when recommended by a doctor, should be made illegal. _____

15. People suffering from incurable disease should have the choice of being put painlessly to death. _____

16. Capitalism is immoral because it exploits the worker by failing to give him full value for his productive labour. _____

17. We should believe without question all that we are taught by the Church. _____

A, B, C,
D, or E

18. A person should be free to take his or her own life, if so desired, without any interference from society. _____

19. Free love between men and women should be encouraged as a means towards mental and physical health. _____

20. Compulsory military training in peace-time is essential for the survival of this country. _____

21. Sex crimes such as rape and attacks on children, deserve more than mere imprisonment; such criminals ought to be flogged or worse. _____

22. A white lie is often a good thing. _____

23. The idea of God is an invention of the human mind. _____

24. The Church should attempt to increase its influence on the life of the nation. _____

25. The laws against abortion should be abolished. _____

26. Most religious people are hypocrites. _____

27. Sex relations except in marriage are always wrong. _____

28. Refugees should be left to fend for themselves. _____

29. It is wrong to punish a man if he helps another country because he prefers it to his own. _____

30. It is just as well that the struggle of life tends to weed out those who cannot stand the pace. _____

31. In taking part in any form of world organization, this country should make certain that none of its independence and power is lost. _____

32. Nowadays, more and more people are prying into matters which do not concern them. _____

33. Jews are as valuable citizens as any other group. _____

A, B, C,
D, or E

34. Our treatment of criminals is too harsh; we should try to cure them, not punish them. _____

35. The Church is the main bulwark opposing the evil trends in modern society. _____

36. There is no harm in travelling constantly without a ticket, if you can get away with it. _____

37. Life is so short that people are justified in enjoying themselves as much as they can. _____

38. An occupation by a foreign power is better than war. _____

39. Christ was divine, wholly or partly in a sense different from other men. _____

40. The Universe was created by God. _____

41. Blood sports, such as fox hunting, are vicious and cruel, and should be forbidden. _____

42. The maintenance of internal order within the nation is more important than ensuring that there is complete freedom for all. _____

Key

For Radicalism, on items 1, 7, 12, 16, 19, 29, 34, 38 count A as 5 points, B as 4 points, C as 3 points, D as 2 points, and E as 1 point. On items 2, 5, 6, 8, 17, 21, 27, 31 count A as 1 point, B as 2 points, C as 3 points, D as 4 points, and E as 5 points. Scores above 48 are in the *radical* direction, scores below 24 are in the *conservative* direction. The further above or below 48 your score is, the more radical or conservative will you be.

For tendermindedness, on items 11, 13, 14, 24, 27, 33, 34, 35, 38, 39, 40, 41 count A as 5 points, etc. On items 3, 4, 5, 7, 9, 10, 12, 15, 18, 19, 20, 22, 23, 26, 28, 30, 32, 36, 37, 42, count A as 1 point, etc. Scores above 96 are in the *tenderminded* direction, scores below 96 are in the *toughminded* direction. The further above or below 96 your score is, the more toughminded or tenderminded will you be.

100

Fem(-inist) fatale?

If some radicalism in general indicates a tendency towards marital dissatisfaction, it would only stand to reason that *feminism*, a branch of radicalism, would add to the troubles within marriage. The very nature of feminism, with its tendency towards confrontation as opposed to accommodation, starts the spark, and this means marital difficulties. Let it also be said at this point that the *emotional manipulation* found in traditional domestic women led toward marital dissatisfaction as well. Again, *extremes* seem to cause the problems.

Feminist or Anti-Feminist Beliefs

Indicate your feelings about each statement by circling your choice: Strongly agree A, Agree B, Don't know C, Disagree D, Strongly disagree E.

1. Men have held power for too long ....   **A B C D E**

2. Beauty contests are degrading to   **A B C D E**
   women...

101

3. Children of working mothers are bound to suffer ....   A   B   C   D   E

4. Wives who don't work should do all the housekeeping ....   A   B   C   D   E

5. Women should be given immediate equality of pay ....   A   B   C   D   E

6. Women should be given preference in hiring and promotion until past injustices are corrected ....   A   B   C   D   E

7. Most men are chauvinists......................   A   B   C   D   E

8. Women are naturally better suited to the job of child-rearing ....   A   B   C   D   E

9. Women should make an effort to be attractive to men................................   A   B   C   D   E

10. Husbands should always do an equal share of household chores ....   A   B   C   D   E

11. Women's Lib will change the world for the better ....   A   B   C   D   E

12. Employers should be free to prefer men if they think the job calls for a man........   A   B   C   D   E

13. Only through following her own career can a woman find fulfilment..................   A   B   C   D   E

14. Women's Libbers are usually just manhaters ....   A   B   C   D   E

15. Equal pay for women is at present an unrealistic aim ....   A   B   C   D   E

16. Men should spend an equal amount of time in child-care duties ....   A   B   C   D   E

17. Chivalry and romance are threatened by Women's Lib....................................   A   B   C   D   E

18. In many respects women have it easier than men already.................................   A   B   C   D   E

Scoring Key

On questions 1, 2, 5, 6, 7, 10, 11, 13 and 16 give 5 points for an A, 4 points for a B, 3 points for a C, 2 points for a D, and 1 point for a E. On questions 3, 4, 8, 9, 12, 14, 15, 17 and 18 give 1 point for an A, 2 points for a B, 3 points for a C, 4 points for a D, and 5 points for an E. Scores above 54 indicate some degree of feminism, scores below 54 some degree of anti-feminism. The further above or below 54, the greater the degree of feminism or anti-feminism.

Masculine-feminine

If women generally seem to have higher neuroticism scores and men higher psychoticism scores, it would seem that perhaps other traits are gender-based as well, at least by general definition in our present society. This next questionnaire, designed by Professor Sandra Bem of Stanford University in California, arbitrarily relates certain traits to typical female behaviour, others to masculine, *all* based not so much on biological reality as the stereotypes in our present Western society.

People are above all people, and it should be clear that each person possesses many items from both the male and female scale. Do these actually correlate? Apparently, the answer is no: masculinity and femininity seem to constitute different dimensions within each sex and are relatively independent of one another.

Masculinity–Femininity Scale

These are descriptions of behaviour which is typical of certain personalities. Answer in each case to what degree this kind of behaviour is characteristic of *you*; is the description nearly always true, often true, doubtful, seldom true, or nearly never true?

	Nearly always	Often		Seldom	Nearly never
1. Acts as a leader	A	B	?	D	E
2. Affectionate	A	B	?	D	E
3. Aggressive	A	B	?	D	E

	Nearly always	Often		Seldom	Nearly never
4. Cheerful	A	B	?	D	E
5. Ambitious	A	B	?	D	E
6. Childlike	A	B	?	D	E
7. Analytical	A	B	?	D	E
8. Compassionate	A	B	?	D	E
9. Assertive	A	B	?	D	E
10. Does not use harsh language	A	B	?	D	E
11. Athletic	A	B	?	D	E
12. Eager to soothe hurt feelings	A	B	?	D	E
13. Competitive	A	B	?	D	E
14. Feminine	A	B	?	D	E
15. Defends own beliefs	A	B	?	D	E
16. Flatterable	A	B	?	D	E
17. Dominant	A	B	?	D	E
18. Gentle	A	B	?	D	E
19. Forceful	A	B	?	D	E
20. Gullible	A	B	?	D	E
21. Has leadership abilities	A	B	?	D	E
22. Loves children	A	B	?	D	E
23. Independent	A	B	?	D	E
24. Loyal	A	B	?	D	E
25. Individualistic	A	B	?	D	E
26. Sensitive to the needs of others	A	B	?	D	E
27. Makes decisions easily	A	B	?	D	E
28. Shy	A	B	?	D	E
29. Masculine	A	B	?	D	E
30. Soft spoken	A	B	?	D	E
31. Self-reliant	A	B	?	D	E
32. Sympathetic	A	B	?	D	E
33. Self-sufficient	A	B	?	D	E
34. Tender	A	B	?	D	E

	Nearly always	Often		Seldom	Nearly never
35. Strong personality	A	B	?	D	E
36. Understanding	A	B	?	D	E
37. Willing to take a stand	A	B	?	D	E
38. Warm	A	B	?	D	E
39. Willing to take risks	A	B	?	D	E
40. Yielding	A	B	?	D	E

Key

For all odd-numbered items, count each A answer 5 points, each B answer 4 points, each ? answer 3 points, each D answer 2 points, and each E answer 1 point. Add these points together to give your *masculinity* score. For all even-numbered items, do the same; this will give you your femininity score. Scores of 60 indicate an average degree of masculinity or femininity; scores above are masculine or feminine, scores below are undifferentiated. The further above or below 60 scores are, the more clear-cut is the identification. When both scores are above 60, you are androgynous.

Androgyny in monogamy

Anybody who combines many traits from both genders is technically known as androgynous – again, from the Greek, *andros* meaning male and *gune* meaning female. A person scoring high in the masculine would be psychologically masculine, whereas someone high in femine items and low in masculine would be in the feminine quadrant. The last quadrant would contain people low on both items, and there is no specific term to describe them. Perhaps 'undifferentiated' is the best term to use.

Androgyny for harmony

Professor Bernard Mustin has good news in this liberated day and age: the happiest couples seemed to be those where both parties leaned toward androgyny. In this respect, then,

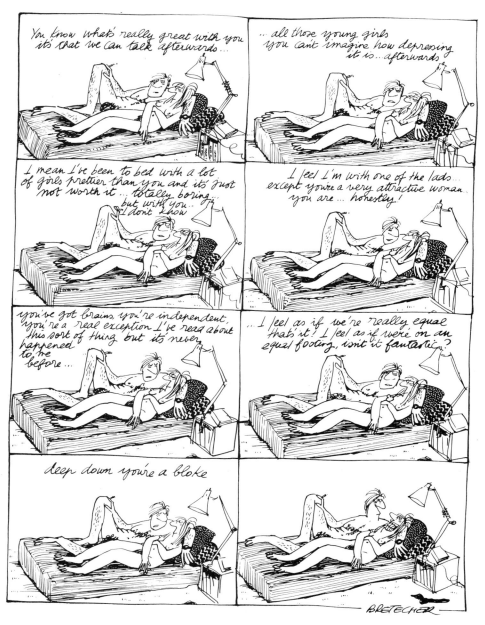

homogamy is indeed the happy medium for marriage; next down the line in satisfaction were those couples high in differentiation. The least happy were those found in the fourth quadrant of undifferentiation, which should come as no surprise to anyone. However, it is also interesting to note that if there were going to be differentiation, the best situation would be the man differentiated or else androgynous.

Generally speaking, all these studies have led to two main conclusions: Neither homogamy nor asymmetry in gender behaviour seems to be the answer to happiness; it is more a question of reflecting on patterns current in the general population. In other words men and women were happier in marriage if their personalities went in the same direction as the general population. If more women are tenderminded than men, it is better for women to be more tenderminded in marriage. But the most important conclusion has to do not with your partner but with *yourself*: your marriage will be as happy as you are; it will be what you bring into the union. Happy does as happy is, and perhaps that is as true in marriage as it is anywhere else in life.

Happiness and unhappiness in marriage

Scientists agree that a happy marriage is not necessarily one which is free from problems. All marriages, happy and unhappy, have to face basic challenges – setting goals, making decisions, and solving problems – which often change very little over the years. The vital difference between happy and unhappy marriages lies in the degree to which both partners agree on what their problems are and work to solve them together.

These findings emerge from a long-term investigation into the dynamics of marriage conducted by Professor Clifford H. Swenson and his colleagues at Purdue University, Indiana. Today, Swenson points out, the average married couple can expect 48 years of marriage before being separated by death of one of the partners. Twenty-five of those years will be spent together after the last child has left home. In his studies, which are still continuing, Swenson is concerned to measure the quality of satisfaction in marriage throughout all the stages of married life.

A commitment to happiness

In Swenson's opinion, the basic ingredient of a happy marriage is not the absence of problems, but the commitment you bring to the marriage in the first place:

> Commitment is getting married and staying married because of the personal characteristics of the other person. I think there is a tendency to transcend problems when there is that bond that is basic for resolving them.

In a survey which included both happily and unhappily married couples, Swenson measured their degree of commitment by analysing the answers to two questions:

A. What were your reasons for your decisions to marry him/her?

B. Why do you think your marriage has lasted as long as it has?

Highly committed couples gave mutual admiration for each other's personal qualities as the reason for deciding to get married. They cited an ever-deepening companionship, friendship and love as the main reason for the continuation of marriage. Couples with a low level of commitment had decided on marriage for largely non-personal reasons: 'it was the natural thing to do', 'thought he could provide well', or because 'she could have my children, keep my house and look after me in my old age'. As reasons for the marriage lasting, these couples tended to talk of financial necessity, the needs of the children, or simply of having no other choice.

Comparing the two groups, Swenson found that couples with low commitment had more marriage problems in general, particularly in problem-solving and decision-making, dealing with relatives and in-laws, and in expressing affection. His conclusion is that commitment – and learning how to express and enact commitment – is the most important factor affecting marriage problems. More specifically, conscious efforts to become aware of your partner's unique qualities, to discuss with him or her the importance of problems as they arise, and to share equally in solving them, are likely to increase the satisfaction both of you will experience in marriage.

Ref: 'Marriages that endure', *Families Today*, Volume I, pp. 249–85, Ed. Eunice Corfman, NIMH Science Monographs 1, 1979 Rockville, Maryland.
Fiore, A. and Swenson, C. H., Analysis of love relationships in functional and dysfunctional marriages. *Psychological Reports*, 1977, *40*, 707–714.

5

Sex and marital satisfaction

And now we come to the perennial question of the role that sex plays in marriage. Most people would agree that good sex is essential to a good marriage. Even though a small percentage of the population withdraws into homosexual and lesbian groups, the majority still seeks most of its sexual satisfaction in marriage. But what is good sex? Do men and women have different expectations of the sexual relationship within marriage? What are the factors which make for a fulfilling sexual union between a man and a woman?

Let's look at the question of homogamy – similarity – first. It appears that when it comes to sex the rule of homogamy completely breaks down. Whereas for personality, intelligence, social background and the like, homogamy seems essential to a healthy relationship, it is not so with sex. In fact it is just the opposite.

We have already mentioned Plato's picture of the ideal human relationship. He described a complete human being as being represented by a circle cut in half, one half representing the male, the other half representing the female – the point being that by complementing each other they achieve unity and wholeness. Modern research suggests that Plato was right: complementarity is essential to sexual happiness. To understand which men and which women are most likely to complement each other, we must understand more about the sexuality of the particular man and woman in question.

A famous epigram has it that marriage is so popular because it combines the maximum of temptation and the maximum of

'I love the idea of there being two sexes, don't you?'

opportunity. Equally, there's an old Victorian saying that men marry in order to have sex, but women have sex in order to marry. George Bernard Shaw sharpened the paradox when he said 'What is virtue but the trade unionism of the married?' The suggestion in all this is that sex means more to men than to women, and that marriage allows them far greater opportunities for sex than they would otherwise have. The price they have to pay is marriage. Women, on the other hand, were thought to be more interested in love, and in the companionship and stability that marriage provided, than in sex. The price they have to pay is the humiliation of the marriage bed.

Most people today would consider these stereotypes absurd, claiming that attitudes and sexual practices have changed enormously since Victorian times. However, what is interesting to me as a social scientist is whether or not there may still be some truth in these old adages, whether or not they have any bearing on the way we live today, whether or not, in fact, our sexual attitudes and behaviours have changed significantly.

112

Sex and personality

We are fortunate when it comes to looking at the relationship between sexual behaviour and personality, since we know a great deal about both. First, let us consider the difference between extraverts and introverts. As we have seen, extraverts tend to be sociable, lively, outgoing, 'sensation-seeking' people, who are easily bored by repetitive stimulation and seek novelty above all. They change jobs frequently, move often and show less 'brand loyalty' than their more introverted peers. They also need strong sensory stimulation, so that they tend to thrive on hot, spicy foods, strong drinks, bright lights and loud noises.

The need for this strong stimulation derives from the physiology of their brains. Within the brain is a system responsible for, among other functions, the sensation of appetite and satiety. This system responds to external stimuli by putting the body into a state of arousal.

The term arousal is a technical one, referring to a series of physical changes, including an increase in heart-rate, dilation of the pupil, rapid, shallow breathing and changes in the digestive system. When we're involved in what we are doing, for example taking an exam, or watching an exciting tennis match, our system is in a state of high arousal. When we're not very engaged in what we are doing we are in a state of low arousal.

Arousal can be measured by the amount of electrical activity taking place in the brain. Extraverts are characterized by a habitually low state of arousal and so they seek to offset this by strong stimuli. Introverts, on the other hand, are characterized by a perpetually high state of arousal so they try to offset this by avoiding strong stimuli and new situations. Most people seek average levels of arousal, somewhere in between, neither too high nor too low. But, rather than getting too involved in an analysis of the complicated chemistry of the brain, suffice it to say that the needs of introverts and extraverts are different, that these needs have a physiological basis and lead to different kinds of behaviour.

114

So how would this apply to sexual behaviour differences between extraverts and introverts? The predictions are not difficult to make. In general:

1 Extraverts will have intercourse at an earlier age than introverts.

2 Extraverts will have intercourse more frequently than introverts.

3 Extraverts will have intercourse with more partners.

4 Extraverts will have intercourse in more different positions than introverts.

5 Extraverts will indulge in more varied sexual behaviour outside intercourse.

6 Extraverts will indulge in longer precoital loveplay than introverts.

7 Extraverts will become more quickly bored with given types of sexual stimulation than will introverts.

Testing sexual arousal

There is much evidence to support these predictions. Most of the studies have been based on verbal behaviour, in other words, on what people have said, but some of them have been based on experiments. As a matter of fact, we conducted one experimental study in our own laboratories. The point of the study was to test prediction number seven, above, and it was designed in the following way. The subjects were all male, and we saw them individually on three separate days. Each day we showed them three four-minute films which could be classified as hard-core pornography. Each of the films was followed by four minutes of rest, so that the entire experience for the man lasted for only about twenty minutes. Now the films themselves were composites, made up of pieces of longer pornographic films and put together in such a way that each film simply showed the same kind of sexual activity over and over again, but performed by different actors. One film might show conventional sexual intercourse, another oral sex with both partners participating, one in which the woman is performing oral sex on the man and one in which the man is performing cunnilingus on the woman. We measured the sexual excitement of each subject as he watched the films, by putting a strain gauge around his penis and measuring the extent of his erection. Half of our subjects were very extraverted, and half were introverted. Half were stable and half were unstable. But it turned out that the emotional stability of the subjects made no difference in the results, so we will simply refer to different reactions between the introverted and the extraverted men.

On the basis of our seventh prediction we would expect that extraverts would tire of the film more quickly than introverts because of the lack of novelty, and we would expect that this loss of interest would be reflected by a lowering of the amount of erection shown. And, indeed, this is what we found. For each film, introverts preserved their original erections much more readily than did extraverts. This was true for all the films shown on one day, and for all three days. So, from the first film on the first day to the last film on the last day, there was a tremendous decrease in the amount of erection with which the extraverted males reacted to the film, but hardly any decrease in responsiveness among the introverted males. I mention this study simply to demonstrate that we are not relying only on what people say when they talk about their sexual responses. We have tested some of our hypotheses experimentally, and so are not dependent on the subjective verbal responses of the subjects in question. Unfortunately, on the test we ran, we were only able to test males.

Extraverts, introverts and sexual activity
Another study which is relevant to our predictions was conducted in Germany and used a large number of students.

116

Some of the results of this study are the following: When asked whether or not they had engaged in petting by the age of 17, 40 per cent of the extraverted males said yes while only 16 per cent of the introverted males said yes. For females asked the same question, 24 per cent of the extraverts said yes and 15 per cent of the introverted females. These differences held up even when the same students were tested at different ages. Of the extraverted males, 21 per cent had coitus at 17 while only 5 per cent of the introverted ones had had coitus. For the females, 8 per cent of the extraverts had had intercouse by the age of 17 as against only 4 per cent of the introverted women.

The average frequency of coitus per month was twice as high for the extraverted males and females as for the introverted ones. For the unmarried students, the number of coitus partners in the last twelve months was over four for 25 per cent of the extraverted males, but over four for only 7 per cent of the introverted males; it was over four partners for 17 per cent of the extraverted females and only 4 per cent of the introverted females.

And, finally, this study found that the experience of orgasm was almost always claimed twice as often by extraverted women as by introverted ones. Another important factor, when it comes to orgasm, is neuroticism. Women high on the neuroticism scale tend to have more difficulty in achieving orgasm than do women who are lower on this scale.

The findings that we've looked at so far give us a broad, general measure of people's sexual activity. Male or female, the extravert – the outgoing sensation seeker – will have more sexual experience with more partners than the male or female introvert – the more stable type of personality.

However, we need to know more, and in more detail, about people's sexual behaviour. In particular we need to know how important the sexual side of married life is to overall marital happiness. Moreover, people differ from one another in their sexual needs, attitudes and experience, as well as in their personality traits. So, most people would want to ask which combinations of sexual attitudes and experience, and which combinations of personality types, are most likely to result in sexual satisfaction within marriage.

Let me deal immediately with the relationship between sexual and marital satisfaction. *All* studies agree that sexual dissatisfaction is a major symptom of a marriage in trouble. This is only to be expected – although you may be surprised to know that in one widely accepted list of the ten most important issues for *all* marriages, sexual satisfaction ranks fifth in priority behind day-to-day questions of communication.

Individual needs

The word 'dissatisfaction', though, is a very broad category. In our own survey we devised a questionnaire designed to measure individual sexual attitudes, needs, and satisfaction and their relationship to different types of personality. You may like to fill in the questionnaire for yourself. It will provide an indication of your levels of libido – the psychic drive towards sexual experience – the degree of your sexual satisfaction, and their relationship to your personality type – whether extravert, introvert, neurotic or psychotic. Remember, there are no 'good' or 'bad' answers, simply differences. In the light of the results of the questionnaire you will know something more about yourself, and about the sort of person with whom you are more likely to find sexual satisfaction.

Sexual Attitude Inventory

Read each statement carefully, then circle the YES or the NO answer, depending on your views. If you cannot decide, circle the ? reply. Please answer *every* question. There are no right or wrong answers. Don't think too long over each question; try to give an immediate answer which represents your *feeling* on each issue. Some questions are similar to others; there are good reasons for getting at the same attitude in slightly different ways.

1. The opposite sex will respect you more if you are not too familiar with them.   Yes   ?   No

2. Sex without love ('impersonal sex') is highly unsatisfactory.   Agree   ?   Disagree

3. Conditions have to be just right to get me sexually excited.   Yes   ?   No

4. All in all I am satisfied with my sex life.   Yes   ?   No

5. Virginity is a girl's most valuable possession.   Yes   ?   No

6. I think only rarely about sex.   Yes   ?   No

7. Sometimes it has been a problem to control my sex feelings.   Yes   ?   No

8. I get a pleasant feeling from touching my sexual parts.   Yes   ?   No

9. I have been deprived sexually.   Yes   ?   No

10. I do not need to respect a person or love them, in order to enjoy petting and/or intercourse with them.   Yes   ?   No

11. Frankly, I prefer people of my own sex.   Yes   ?   No

12. Sex contacts have never been a problem to me.   True   ?   False

13. Sexual feelings are sometimes unpleasant to me.   True   ?   False

14. Something is lacking in my sex life.   Yes   ?   No

15. My sex behaviour has never caused me any trouble.   True   ?   False

16. My love life has been disappointing.   Yes   ?   No

17. I never had many dates.   True   ?   False

18. It wouldn't bother me if the person I married was not a virgin.   True   ?   False

119

19. It doesn't take much to get me
    sexually excited.   True   ?   False

20. My parent's influence has inhibited
    me sexually.   Yes   ?   No

21. Thoughts about sex disturb me more
    than they should.   True   ?   False

22. I think about sex almost every day.   Yes   ?   No

23. One should not experiment with sex
    before marriage.   Agree ?   Disagree

24. I get excited sexually very easily.   Yes   ?   No

25. The thought of a sex orgy is disgust-
    ing to me.   Yes   ?   No

26. It is better not to have sex relations
    until you are married.   True   ?   False

27. I find the thought of a coloured sex
    partner particularly exciting.   Yes   ?   No

28. I like to look at sexy pictures.   Yes   ?   No

29. My conscience bothers me too much.   Yes   ?   No

30. Sometimes sexual feelings overpow-
    er me.   Yes   ?   No

31. I enjoy petting.   Yes   ?   No

32. I worry a lot about sex.   Yes   ?   No

33. Seeing a person nude doesn't interest
    me.   True   ?   False

34. Sometimes the woman should be
    sexually aggressive.   Yes   ?   No

35. Sex jokes disgust me.   Yes   ?   No

36. I believe in taking my pleasures
    where I find them.   Yes   ?   No

37. Young people should be allowed out
    at night without being too closely
    checked.   Yes   ?   No

38. I would especially protect my children from contacts with sex. Yes ? No

39. I have been involved with more than one sex affair at the same time. Yes ? No

40. It is all right to seduce a person who is old enough to know what they are doing. Yes ? No

41. I like to look at picture of nudes. Yes ? No

42. If I had the chance to see people making love, without being seen, I would take it. Yes ? No

43. Pornographic writing should be allowed to be freely published. Yes ? No

44. Prostitution should be legally permitted. Yes ? No

45. Decisions about abortion should be the concern of no one but the woman concerned. Yes ? No

46. There are too many immoral plays on TV. Yes ? No

47. I had some bad sexual experiences when I was young. Yes ? No

48. There should be no censorship, on sexual grounds, of plays and films. Agree ? Disagree

49. Sex is far and away my greatest pleasure. Yes ? No

50. Sexual permissiveness threatens to undermine the entire foundation of civilized society. Yes ? No

51. Absolute faithfulness to one partner throughout life is nearly as silly as celibacy. Yes ? No

52. The present preoccupation with sex in our society has been largely created by films, newspapers, television and advertising. True ? False

121

53. I would enjoy watching my usual partner having intercourse with someone else.　　Yes　?　No

54. I would vote for a law that permitted polygamy.　　Yes　?　No

55. Even though one is having regular intercourse, masturbation is good for a change.　　Yes　?　No

56. I would prefer to have a new sex partner every night.　　Yes　?　No

57. I make lots of vocal noises during intercourse.　　Yes　?　No

58. Sex is more exciting with a stranger.　　Yes　?　No

59. To me few things are more important than sex.　　True　?　False

60. My sex partner completely satisfies all my physical needs.　　Yes　?　No

61. Sex is not all that important to me.　　True　?　False

62. I find it easy to tell my sex partner what I like or don't like about their love-making.　　Yes　?　No

63. I would like my sex partner to be more expert and experienced.　　Yes　?　No

64. I sometimes feel like scratching and biting my partner during intercourse.　　Yes　?　No

65. No one has ever been able to satisfy me sexually.　　True　?　False

66. I feel less sexually competent than my friends.　　Yes　?　No

67. Group sex appeals to me.　　Yes　?　No

68. The thought of an illicit relationship appeals to me.　　Yes　?　No

69. I am afraid of sexual relationships.　　Yes　?　No

70. I prefer my partner to dictate the rules of the sexual game. Yes ? No

71. Genitals of the opposite sex are aesthetically unpleasing. Agree ? Disagree

72. I object to four-letter swear words being used in mixed company. Yes ? No

73. The idea of 'wife swapping' is extremely distasteful to me. True ? False

74. My own sex are more selfish in their love-making than members of the opposite sex. Yes ? No

75. Some forms of love-making are disgusting to me. Yes ? No

76. It is right that man should be the dominant partner in a sex relationship. Yes ? No

Please circle the correct answer

77. If you were invited to see a 'blue' film, you would:
(a) accept (b) refuse.

78. If you were offered a highly pornographic book, you would:
(a) accept it (b) reject it.

79. If you were invited to take part in an orgy, you would:
(a) take part (b) refuse.

80. Ideally, would you prefer to have intercourse:
(a) never, (b) once a month, (c) once a week, (d) twice a week, (e) 3–5 times a week, (f) every day, (g) more than once a day.

81. Rate the habitual strength of your sexual desire from 10 (absolutely overwhelming and all-embracing) to 1 (very weak and almost non-existent).
Rating_____

82. Rate the strength of the influences that inhibit you sexually (moral, aesthetic, religious, etc.) from 10 (terribly strong, completely inhibiting) to 1 (very weak and almost non-existent).
Rating_____

Key – Libido Scale

Score 1 point for each of the following questions answered 'Yes': 8, 18, 22, 24, 27, 28, 30, 36, 39, 40, 41, 42, 43, 44, 48, 51, 53, 54, 55, 67, 68.
Score 1 point for each of the following questions answered 'No': 1, 2, 5, 6, 23, 25, 26, 46, 50, 72, 73.
Questions 52, 77, 78, and 79: Score 1 point if you endorse 'a'.
Question 80: Score 1 point if you endorse e, f or g.
Top score is 36, bottom score 0. Average male score would be about 23, average female score 16.

Key – Sexual Satisfaction Score

Score 1 point for each of the following questions answered 'Yes': 4, 15, 60. Score 1 point for each of the following questions answered 'No': 9, 11, 13, 14, 16, 20, 21, 29, 32, 65, 66, 69, 71.
A score of 16 shows maximum satisfaction with your sex life; a score of 0 shows maximum dissatisfaction.

Key – Masculinity Scale

Score 1 point for each of the following questions answered 'Yes': 7, 8, 10, 17, 19, 22, 24, 27, 28, 31, 34, 36, 37, 41, 42, 43, 44, 48, 49, 51, 53, 54.
Score 1 point for each of the following questions answered 'No': 2, 3, 12, 13, 25, 29, 33, 35, 38, 45, 47, 52.
A score of 34 points would be the highest possible 'masculine' score, a score of 0 the lowest. A score of 17 would be intermediate, but of course males have a higher mean than females – 22 as opposed to 14.

Libido

The first measure we deal with is that of libido, which is the psychological term for sex-drive. What sort of attitudes do we find in an individual with a *high* libido? Although there are obviously exceptions, a person with a high libido would tend to think as follows: It would not bother me if the person I married was not a virgin. It doesn't take much to get me sexually excited. I get pleasant feelings from touching my sexual parts. I think of sex almost every day. I like to look at sexy pictures.

Sometimes sexual feelings are overpowering for me. I enjoy petting. I believe in taking pleasure where I can. I have been involved with more than one affair at a time. It is okay to seduce a person who is old enough to know what he or she is doing. If I had a chance to watch people making love, I would take it. Publication of pornography should not be restricted. Prostitution should be legal. Films and plays should not be censored on the grounds of sex. Sex is far and away my greatest pleasure. Faithfulness to a partner is silly. Celibacy is silly. I would enjoy watching my partner have sex with someone else. I would vote for a law permitting polygamy. I enjoy intercourse regularly, but feel that masturbation is good for a change. I would prefer a new partner every night. Group sex appeals to me. The thought of illicit relationships excites me. Sex is the most important part of marriage. I like to watch pornographic movies and read pornographic books. I would accept an invitation to an orgy if offered. My sexual desire is very strong.

On the other hand, someone with a low libido would tend to express the following attitudes: The opposite sex will respect you more if you are not too familiar. 'Impersonal love' is highly unsatisfactory. Virginity is a girl's most valuable possession. I rarely think of sex. I don't like to see necking in public. There are some things I wouldn't do with anyone. One shouldn't experiment with sex before marriage. The thought of a sex orgy disgusts me. I don't like dirty jokes. There's too much sex on TV. Sexual permissiveness threatens to undermine civilized society. Sex is not all that important. I object to four-letter words in mixed company. Wife-swapping is very distasteful to me. Some forms of love-making are disgusting.

Reading through the list will give you an idea of the respective *extremes* in taste of the person with high, and with low libido. There are, of course, very strong sex differences, with males in general scoring higher on libido than do females, but there is also a certain amount of overlap. Some women have a stronger libido than the average male, and some males have a weaker libido than the average female.

Keep it in perspective: sexual satisfaction

The next measure is of sexual satisfaction. I should say at once that sexual satisfaction is completely independent of libido. It is very possible for a person with a high libido to be as satisfied with his or her sex life as a person with a low libido. Study after study has shown that this conclusion is essentially correct. So, regardless of how high or low the individual libido, a person who is satisfied with his or her sex life would tend to express these attitudes: I feel at ease with the opposite sex. My partner satisfies all my physical needs. It is easy for me to tell my partner how I feel about his or her love-making. I am satisfied with my sex life. I like the naked body. My sexual behaviour has never caused me any trouble. I enjoy lengthy precoital love play.

Someone very dissatisfied with his or her sex life would tend to have attitudes such as: I have been deprived sexually. Sex feelings bother me sometimes. Something is lacking in my sex life. My love life has been disappointing. My parents' influence has inhibited me sexually. I feel guilty about sex sometimes. I am uncomfortable with the opposite sex. I worry about sex a lot. I feel less sexually competent than my friends. I'm afraid of close sexual relationships. I don't like to be touched.

You should be able to see how you fit on the scales of libido and sexual satisfaction by scoring your answers to the preceding questionnaire and seeing how your answers fit in to this general scheme.

Libido and heredity

Both personality and genetic factors affect one's degree of libido and amount of sexual satisfaction. This shouldn't be surprising, since personality itself is strongly determined by genetic factors. We have analysed the behaviour of identical and fraternal twins and come up with strong evidence to support this view. When it comes to sexual satisfaction, for example, almost 40 per cent of all the observed differences in the attitudes expressed by males can be accounted for by heredity. In other words, the closer the genetic similarity between males, the more likely they are to report similar levels of sexual satisfaction. In the case of females, the part played by heredity is, again, about 40 per cent.

Cultural pressures

However, when it comes to libido and the influence of heredity upon it, we see a marked difference between men and women. Heredity plays a much larger role in determining the degree of libido in men than it does in women. Why? Because, apparently, cultural influences modulate a woman's inherited sexual instincts. Most societies at most times in history have placed a high value on sexual modesty in women. And, although it's certainly true that, in the West, free expression of female sexuality is now broadly accepted, it is *not* true, for example, of Islamic societies. Even in the West the so-called sexual revolution is less than 20 years old. It will take much longer for the relaxation of social attitudes towards female

127

sexuality to show through in the expressed attitudes of women (at least Western women) in general.

Masculine and feminine

The third scale we need to take a look at is the masculinity scale. This scale weighs those traits which most clearly differentiate between men and women. It is fairly similar to the libido scale, and, just as men score higher on libido, so will they score higher on masculinity than will women. I include this scale simply as a point of interest to the reader who may be curious to see how his or her scores on it compare with others. Once again, there is no 'bad' or 'good' when it comes to these scores. High or low scores are simply characteristic of a given person. There is absolutely no reason why a man or woman should score near the mean. Any score can be compatible with contentment and marital happiness. You might like to keep track of your score on this scale because we will refer to it again in Chapter 6.

Personality: psychoticism

Now we come to the question of how these factors are related to personality. If you have completed the personality questionnaires in Chapter 4, you will already know about the three scales of personality measurement: introversion – extraversion, neuroticism (N), and psychoticism (P). And you will know, too, that terms like 'neurotic' and 'psychotic' are used here in a special sense. They are *not* related to medically diagnosed neurosis or psychosis. Let's look at psychoticism (P) first. High-P scorers are opposed to the conventions of society. They would like to do away with marriage; they approve of polygamy; they think it is reasonable to seduce any willing person old enough to know what he or she is doing; they approve of premarital sex. They have what they would call a realistic view of sex. They think that romantic love is an illusion, that tenderness in sex is not important, that faithfulness in marriage is silly. They believe in taking sex where they can find it and they would not be disturbed if their partner had sex with someone else. High-P scorers are permissive, they feel that pornography should be freely available, that orgies are fine, that sex play among children is harmless. All in all, high-P scorers emerge as advocates of impersonal, permissive sexual practices. They feel that social laws governing marriage should be abandoned. Basically they feel that 'all's fair in love and war'.

It is interesting to note, however, that they are not particularly satisfied with their sex lives. There is some indication that they feel nervous with the opposite sex, and that they feel guilty about sex itself. They don't like people to touch them, for example, and they admit to feeling guilty about sexual experiences.

Extraversion–introversion

Now for the differences between the attitudes endorsed by extraverts and introverts. In general, extraverts have happy sex lives. They have many friends, they feel relaxed with the opposite sex, they are highly sexed and have had intercourse early in their lives, and often from then on. They get sexually excited easily, they think about sex almost every day and they have no trouble in expressing these strong sexual feelings. Their attitude in a sexual relationship is aggressive and overt. They often like to scratch and bite their partner, for example. They usually consider faithfulness in marriage silly, they have been involved in more than one affair at a time, and they would gladly join in an orgy, if invited. They are completely hedonistic and they believe in taking their pleasures where they find them. Their sexual development has been less troubled than that of high-P scorers. They discuss sex openly with their partners, they love to be touched, their religious beliefs don't interfere with their sexual pleasure, they like to make love with the lights on. Both male and female extraverts are animal-like in their sexuality, unembarrassed, and uninhibited, but without the anti-social and conflicting feelings shown by the high-P scorer. Extraverts share the high libido of the high-P scorer, but they also have high scores on sexual satisfaction.

As opposed to the extravert, introverts typically score low for libido – but this, as we have seen, bears no relation to the level of sexual satisfaction expressed.

'Oh no, the neighbours never complain. It turns them on.'

Neuroticism

Emotionally unstable people (the high-N scorers), on the other hand, often find sex disturbing. They feel guilty about it, and can't discuss sex openly with their partner. They are often nervous with the opposite sex and worry about sex a lot. They are highly sexed and consider sex their greatest pleasure. Physical attractiveness is very important to them, as is sex, but thinking about sex makes them nervous. They get excited easily and believe in taking their pleasures where they can find them, but they are not satisfied with their sex lives. They feel that they have been deprived sexually, that there is something abnormal about their desires. They sometimes feel hostile toward their partner and would like to humiliate him or her. They are excited by the thought of illicit relationships, and they are bothered by what they consider to be perverted sexual thoughts.

Interpretation

So, what does our questionnaire tell us? We can say that high libido is shown by high-P scorers, high-N scorers and extraverts. That leaves low libido for the more stable kind of person, the introvert, and the person who has a strong conscience – or what psychologists sometimes talk of as the superego. When it comes to sexual satisfaction, the high libido of the somewhat unstable N and high-P scorer coincides with a lack of sexual satisfaction. The high libido of the extravert is linked to high sexual satisfaction.

Homogamy for sex

And what about the question of homogamy? When it comes to sexual attitudes should like marry like or do opposites attract? As far as libido is concerned, it seems that like marries like. The actual correlation is .43, much higher than the correlation for personality, but not quite as high as the correlation for social attitudes and intelligence. The same is true for sexual satisfaction. Like marries like, the correlation here being almost the same as that for libido, .41. So, for both libido and sexual satisfaction we find a good deal of selection for homogamy. Those with high libidos tend to choose partners with similarly high libidos. Those who are relatively satisfied with their sex lives select partners who are satisfied with their sex lives too. It is interesting, though, that male sexual satisfaction is related to the strength of the female's libido, whereas female sexual satisfaction is quite unrelated to male libido. In other words, men like sexually active female partners, but women have no preference one way or the other.

The sexually compatible marriage

There is one additional study that corroborates our finding that men and women with similar degrees of libido tend to marry each other. In this study married couples were exposed to a variety of erotic stimuli and their reactions were recorded. The degree of arousal between spouses was very similar. They also agreed on which of the material they were shown should be censored, especially for teenagers. So, as we've seen before, their social attitudes as well as their libidinous impulses are similar. It's interesting to note that in this study we found that 'authoritarians', people who are considered tough-minded and conservative, reported both greater arousal and greater restrictiveness. (This may shed some light on Victorian sexual attitudes; to the nineteenth-century man, the sight of a female ankle under the hem of a long dress was an erotic stimulus.)

We would expect sexual satisfaction in both men and women to correlate positively with marital satisfaction, and indeed it does. It is hard to imagine that there are many marriages where sexual satisfaction is high and marital satisfaction is low, at least for any period of time. On the other hand, sexual satisfaction accounts for only 25 per cent of the factors people report as helping to make their marriages happy. Good sex, however, remains crucial to a good marriage: when one partner reports that he or she is sexually satisfied in a marriage, his or her partner reports high overall marital satisfaction. So, both directly and indirectly, good sex makes for a good marriage.

What is the best match between libido scores for each partner? As we saw, males in general have higher libido scores than females: on average the male score is at least twelve points higher than that of the female. Now, according to our studies, marital satisfaction is greatest when the difference between

'He's mild-mannered, bookish and as randy as hell.'

133

libido scores is only three or four points. Problems occur when the male libido is too high relative to that of the female, and this is the case in most marriages because, in the population at large, the average male libido is so much higher than the female. If, as I suggested, cultural forces – traditional morality – have repressed the female libido, then the fact that, in the West, women are being encouraged to accept and develop their sexual instincts will be all for the good. Such a trend will close the gap between the male and female libido difference, and pave the way to more compatible satisfying sex between marriage partners.

Satisfaction
So much for libido. What about the other characteristic we were measuring, sexual satisfaction? On the whole, the males we studied were slightly higher in sexual satisfaction than were the females, leading men to see a higher degree of marital satisfaction than women. For the women, though, the story is very different. Women achieved the optimal degree of marital satisfaction only when they were considerably higher than their husbands on the sexual satisfaction scale. This creates a difficult situation: it seems necessary for the women to achieve much higher sexual satisfaction scores than the males. But this runs counter to what happens in the population in general, where men tend to have higher sexual satisfaction scores than women, as well as in the marriages of the couples we observed, where, again, men reported higher sexual satisfaction. The best advice I can offer is that women should try to increase their own sexual satisfaction scores, just as they should be encouraged to increase their score on libido.

Sexual behaviour
So far, we have been discussing sexual *attitudes*. But what of sexual behaviour itself? Since we've established that, in general, men have higher libidos than women, then we might expect that men would prefer practically all sexual practices

more than women. Also, because men tend to be higher on the extraversion and psychoticism scales while women are higher on neuroticism, we would expect men, in general, to be more likely to enjoy unconventional sexual practices and positions. Both of these suppositions are fully supported by large-scale studies made in England and Germany. The following table gives figures for sexual practices liked and preferred by men and women respectively, standardized at a figure of 100 for men who enjoy intercourse with foreplay. You will see that women like and enjoy this most of all, although their enjoyment of it is less than it is for men.

When we come to the more unconventional sexual practices, however, strong differences emerge. For example, males like fellatio just as much as ordinary intercourse, but only 23 per cent of the women questioned liked it. The same holds true for the combination of fellatio and cunnilingus. Here 80 per cent of the men questioned liked it while only 30 per cent of the women did.

Sexual Practices *liked* and *preferred* by men and women respectively

	Men	Women
Intercourse with foreplay	100	89
Fellatio	99	23
'69'	80	30
Manual stimulation of woman	70	66
Manual stimulation of man	63	30
Cunnilingus	61	54
Anal intercourse	9	7
Sadism	2	0
Masochism	2	0

Both men and women like manual stimulation of the woman to the same degree, but – surprisingly perhaps – manual stimulation of the man by the woman was enjoyed by men much more than by women. Men favour cunnilingus slightly more than women. When it comes to anal intercourse, sadism and masochism, men are just slightly more in favour of these than women, but these findings are probably not very reliable since verbal answers to the questions about these sensitive areas of sexuality may not be very truthful.

We can draw two conclusions from this study. First, men enjoy unusual sexual practices more than women. Second, both men and women prefer passive sexual activity to active, that is, they prefer to be stimulated rather than stimulate their partner.

Sex and marriage today: a survey

In our own survey of married couples, we included a questionnaire on sexual behaviour within marriage. Before going on to read what we found out, you may like to answer the questions yourself to see how your experience compares with the general picture that emerged.

Sexual Behaviour Inventory

1. About how many times per *month* (assume 30 days per month) have you had sexual intercourse during the last year? (Put down the number that tells the average number *per month.*) _____

2. About how many times *per month* would you prefer to have sexual intercourse? _____

3. Do you think your partner is more or less passionate than you are? Much more ___ somewhat more ___ same ___ somewhat less ___ much less ___

4. Do you sometimes refuse intercourse when your partner desires it? Very frequently ___ frequently ___ sometimes ___ rarely ___ never ___

5. When this happens, what is your attitude? Insistent or irritable ___ displeased but not for too long ___ agreeable and considerate ___

6. How long does intercourse usually last? (Do not count the time of preliminary 'petting'.) Estimate average length of time in minutes. _____

7. In sexual intercourse with your partner do you (men please answer A, women B):
   (A) *FOR MEN* ever experience impotence, i.e. an inability to carry out the act? Never ___ sometimes ___ usually ___ always ___
   (B) *FOR WOMEN* experience an orgasm: i.e. a climax of intense feeling followed by quietude and a feeling of relief? Never ___ sometimes ___ usually ___ always ___

8. How much release or satisfaction do you usually get from sexual intercourse with your partner?
   Entirely complete ___ fairly complete ___ moderate ___ little ___ none ___ am left nervous and unsatisfied ___

9. Do you feel that (men please answer A, women B):
   (A) *FOR MEN*: your wife is over modest or prudish in her attitude towards sex? Yes ___ No ___
   (B) *FOR WOMEN*: your husband is too demanding and overzealous in his attitude towards sex? Yes ___ No ___

10. Did you have intercourse with your partner before marriage?
    Yes ___ No ___

11. Did you have intercourse with any other partners before your first marriage?
    None ___ one ___ two ___ three ___ four ___ five ___ more than five ___

12. Do you frequently experience desire for intercourse with someone other than your partner?
    Very frequently ___ frequently ___ sometimes ___ rarely ___ never ___

13. Was your first intercourse (men please answer A, women B):
    (A) *FOR MEN*: intensely enjoyable ___ satisfactory ___ merely tolerable ___ definitely unsatisfactory ___
    (B) *FOR WOMEN*: enjoyable ___ merely tolerated ___ shocking ___ disgusting ___

14. Do you think your partner is *more* or *less* sexually passionate than you are? Much more ___ somewhat more ___ same ___ somewhat less ___ much less ___

Put one tick before each of the things you find more or less satisfactory in intercourse with your partner, and two ticks before each thing which is decidedly unsatisfactory. Men please answer column **A** only, and women please answer column **B** only.

COLUMN A – Men	COLUMN B – Women
___ 15 . Shows too little enthusiasm	___ 15. Shows too little enthusiasm
___ 16. Vagina too large	___ 16. Penis too large
___ 17. Vagina too small	___ 17. Penis too small

COLUMN A – Men	COLUMN B – Women
— 18. Vagina not moist enough	— 18. Has difficulty in getting an erection
— 19. Cannot always reach an orgasm (climax)	— 19. Has difficulty in keeping an erection
— 20. Never reaches an orgasm	— 20. Cannot always reach an ejaculation
— 21. Too slow in reaching an orgasm	— 21. Never has an ejaculation
— 22. Has orgasm too quickly	— 22. Too slow in reaching an ejaculation
— 23. Wants to go to sleep or get up too soon after orgasm	— 23. Has ejaculation too quickly
— 24. Desires intercourse too frequently	— 24. Wants to withdraw penis too soon after ejaculation
— 25. Desires intercourse too rarely	— 25. Wants to go to sleep or get up too soon after intercourse
— 26. Has too little regard for *my* satisfaction	— 26. Desires intercourse too frequently
— 27. Is too animal-like in her passion	— 27. Desires intercourse too rarely
— 28. Expresses too little tenderness during intercourse	— 28. Has too little regard for *my* satisfaction
— 29. Does not 'pet' enough before beginning intercourse	— 29. Is too animal-like in his passion
— 30. Likes to engage in unnatural practices	— 30. Expresses too little tenderness during intercourse
	— 31. Does not 'pet' enough before beginning intercourse
	— 32. Likes to engage in practices to which I object

Results of the survey

Here is a brief summary of our findings, for men and women, presented in the same order as the questions to which they relate.

We found that the women estimated that they had intercourse 13 times per month, while the men said 15. The women said that they would like to have intercourse 16 times per month, the men thought 19 times per month would be preferable.

On the question of whether or not each partner wanted to have a more passionate mate we found a negative correlation. In other words, if a man wanted a more passionate partner, the woman was likely to want a less passionate one and vice versa.

On the issue of refusing intercourse, the man does so rarely, the woman seldom (the actual difference is less than one point out of five). When this does happen men tend to feel agreeable and considerate about it while women tend to be displeased, but not for too long. How one of the partners reacts to the refusal is no guide to how the other will react.

Men feel that intercourse lasts about 12 minutes while women feel it lasts for about 11 minutes. They agree with each other's judgments here and this finding corresponds with the usual average, of about ten minutes, which is shown by other studies.

We found absolutely no relationship between orgasm and impotence between the spouses. Whether the man is occasionally impotent or not has no bearing on the frequency of orgasm in the woman and vice versa.

Both men and women reported that the satisfaction they get from intercourse is fairly complete, but we found that often one partner may report a high degree of satisfaction while the other reports a relatively small degree of satisfaction.

About a quarter of the men queried felt that their wives were overly modest. Only 17 per cent of the women felt that their husbands were too demanding sexually. Again there was little correlation here. In other words, whether the husband was considered too demanding or not by the wife seemed to have little to do with whether the wife was considered too modest or prudish.

Almost all of the people who answered the questionnaire had had intercourse before marriage. The men reported an average of from two or three pre-marital partners, while for the women it was between one and two partners.

Sometimes men expressed an interest in having intercourse with someone other than their partner, but women rarely did. We found, though, that it is likely that when one partner wants to sleep with someone outside the marriage, the other one wants to also.

On the subject of first intercourse men felt it was satisfactory while women merely tolerated it. Obviously, they disagree on this subject.

Males think their wives are less passionate than themselves; females think their husbands are more passionate and the correlation here is negative. This means that if the woman thinks the man is more passionate than she is, he is likely to think her less passionate. No surprises here.

Finally we come to the long list of possible complaints. We found that, on average, men and women have three complaints about their spouses. In general, the number of complaints seem to be mutual – the more complaints the husbands has, the more complaints the wife is likely to have.

Sex, marriage and satisfaction

Having looked at the evidence, what can we say about sex and marital satisfaction?

Husbands: when men were satisfied with the sex in their marriage, they were satisfied with the marriage. When they desired sex with someone other than their wife, their marital satisfaction was low. Both of these findings are exactly as we would expect them to be.

When men had a lot of complaints about their wife, they reported low marital satisfaction. The same holds if the man thinks that the wife is too prudish. If he reports that she is more passionate than he is, then he tends to be happy in his marriage. Frequency of intercourse shows a slight positive correlation with marital satisfaction. Intercourse before marriage, preferred intercourse frequency, and the enjoyability of first intercourse have no bearing on happiness in marriage.

Wives: the same pattern tends to hold true for women. On the positive side, if the wife is happy with the sex in the marriage she is happy with the marriage. Frequency of intercourse is slighly more important to her than it is to her husband. If she has a lot of complaints about her husband, wants to have sex with someone else, or feels that he is too demanding, then she is not very happy in her marriage. Also if her husband refuses to have intercourse with her, or if he is very upset by her refusal, then she also tends to be unhappy in the marriage.

The best of sex

Marital satisfaction is most complete when the woman reports that her husband is more passionate than he reports her to be. It is the highest when the man refuses intercourse more frequently than the woman. It is the highest when both spouses agree that the other spouse is not too prudish or too demanding. It is the highest when the woman wants to have intercourse more often than does the male, and when she receives more satisfaction from the sex than he does. Marital satisfaction is also high when the man reports that his wife is more passionate than she reports him to be.

Here are a few more incidental findings. High marital satisfaction is reported by:

- the partner who refused intercourse less frequently and was less bothered by his or her mate's refusal

- the partner who recalled the longer time of intercourse and who reported high sexual satisfaction

— the partner who felt that his or her mate was neither too prudish nor too demanding

— the partner with fewer pre-marital sex partners

— the partner with less desire for another sex partner

— the partner with fewer complaints about the other

— the partner who reported the more enjoyable first sex experience.

Summary: sex and marriage

In our studies, we found that sexual behaviour was more important to marital satisfaction than any other factor, including personality and social attitudes. The most important finding were that frequent intercourse and high levels of satisfaction from intercourse were strongly associated with marital satisfaction for both sexes. In contrast, desire for another partner, and numerous complaints about the sexual behaviour of the current spouses were – as we might expect – associated with low marital satisfaction. The more passionate the husband thought his wife, the higher the marital satisfaction for both partners. And – again to be expected – the wife's refusal of intercourse was associated with lower marital satisfaction for both parties. There was very little evidence to suggest that either similarity or marked differences in sexual preferences had any bearing on marital satisfaction.

Happiness, personality, sex

This last finding fits in well with the general conclusions we have found in the areas we have looked at, in the last three chapters. At the beginning of Chapter 3 we asked if there was any general rule for marital satisfaction, such as that like marries like, or that opposites attract. We have seen that, although there are some areas of similarity – particularly for intelligence and social background – there is no consistent evidence for either view. We cannot say that extraverts get on better with other extraverts as marriage partners than with introverts.

What we can say, however, is that individual differences are important. Extraverts tend to be happier than introverts, in marriage as in other areas of life. Equally, emotionally unstable people, and people with high levels of aggression and selfishness, tend to be dissatisfied with marriage, as they are with life in general. Since there is some evidence to suggest that we are to a great extent stuck with the personality we are born with, this view may seem to present a gloomy picture – that we are predestined to enjoy life or not, to experience happiness in marriage or not, according to our genetic inheritance.

However, we can offer some hope to offset the gloom. Married people – at every level – are generally happier than their unmarried counterparts. Moreover, even individual traits – such as neuroticism and psychoticism, or stereotyped masculine or feminine behaviours – which tend to work against marital satisfaction may not be fatal. They are much less so, for example, when the spouses differ along the lines of men and women in the community at large – what we have called the asymmetry theory.

Mention of this difference between the sexes leads us on to consider possible causes for the great differences between the personalities and behaviours of men and women in our society. We have seen these differences at every stage in our investigation. Men and women report different levels of happiness within marriage, and different levels of unhappiness outside it. We have seen, also, differences in personality traits between the sexes and, most marked of all, in sexual preferences. We have noticed, too, differences between male and female behaviour in the world of animals, and wondered, in passing, to what extent human animals retain genetically programmed differences in behaviour. These issues will be dealt with in greater detail in the next two chapters.

Rows, disagreements and the causes of friction in marriage

The worst fault a husband can possibly possess in a marriage is violence, according to wives who were questioned for a magazine survey.

Offered a list of faults that can cause stress and misery in marriage and asked to say how serious each was, almost all women (93%) said that they thought 'violence towards wife' was a very serious fault. The wives, questioned by the Opinion Research Centre for *Woman* magazine, also rated gambling, being a bad father and drinking, as 'very serious'. Six out of ten women were critical of husbands who did not give enough housekeeping money. Three-quarters of the women questioned put unfaithfulness in the 'very serious' category, although elsewhere in the survey only one third reported that sexual fidelity was an important part of a good marriage. This could mean that women who were basically happy in their marriage felt that their husbands' good qualities outweighed the miseries caused by the occasional fling.

How the rows start

Rows between husband and wife are most likely to start over trivial subjects – who forgot to turn out the sitting-room light, or whose turn it is to feed the cat, for example. Disagreements over how to treat the children are another common cause of conflict.

Younger wives are more likely to haggle over visiting the in-laws, or complain that their husband doesn't make enough fuss of them.

'He doesn't give me enough help because he spends too much time and energy on his job,' said one young wife.

Money, too, is a major cause of family rows for the less happily married couples. More than a quarter of the women who say they wouldn't choose the same husband again fight with him over the family budget, compared with only 12 per cent of contented wives.

Sex and conflict

As we might expect, sex is a cause of problems in unhappy marriages. While only 2 per cent of the happy wives said they rowed over sex, 17 per cent of women with less satisfactory marriages found sex sufficiently problematic to fight about. Sex problems in marriage have been found to be both the cause and the symptom of a lack of communication between partners. Amercian studies have shown that three out of five women in unhappy marriages and two out of every five men said their sex life had been miserable for about a year before they decided their marriage was in trouble. The link between sex difficulties and unhappy marriages is found both in new marriages and long-established ones of up to 20 years.

Ref: A. Griffiths, *Family Law* (Journal) vol. II 1980, p. 25.

Why the rows start

	Total %
Little arguments which grow	27
Disagreements over how to treat kids	26
Budgeting for expenses and bills	15
Feeling he doesn't appreciate me	15
Visiting in-laws	14
Housekeeping money	11
Him not helping in house	10
Deciding what TV programme to watch	9
His being jealous of other men	9
Wife wanting to get a job	8
Wife being jealous of other women	6
What to do in leisure time	6
Unsatisfactory sex life	5
His not taking an interest in wife's life	4
Temperamentally incompatible	4
Wife not taking enough interest in his work	1
None of these	14

The most important faults

	All Wives %
Hitting or beating his wife	100
Gambling	97
Being a bad father	97
Drinking too much	97
Not giving wife enough housekeeping money	97
Being selfish and inconsiderate	96
Unfaithfulness	95
Being mean about money	93
Lacking in tenderness	84
Being lazy	83
Being too domineering	83
Having a bad temper	82
Keeping income secret from wife	77
Being boring	76
Nagging	72
No sense of humour	71
Not taking wife out enough	67
Being pompous	64
Not strong-willed enough	62
Not wanting sex often enough	61
Spending all his time glued to TV	55
Going out alone leaving wife at home	53
Spending too much time and energy on job	51
Not ambitious enough	48
Wanting sex too often	45
Not being helpful around home	40
Too ambitious	36
Too good-looking	15
Not good-looking enough	2

Opinion Research Centre, Survey for *Woman* magazine, 1978

6

Why can't a woman be more like a man?

Most people would agree that there are clear differences between the social roles and attitudes expected of males and females. This is true, not only in the Western world, but in most, if not all, other cultures as well. These expectations go far beyond the obvious physical differences, taking in day-to-day details of activities and behaviour that have nothing to do with the biological facts of human reproduction. For some years now, the argument has raged as to whether the difference between 'masculine' and 'feminine' roles are purely the result of powerful social pressures to conform, or whether there is some innate genetic programme which does produce different behaviours for men and women.

In previous chapters we have already seen a good number of differences between the sexes as revealed in psychological surveys and questionnaires. In Chapter 5, I included a questionnaire on masculinity–feminity containing 34 questions on which there are the greatest differences between the two sexes. Readers who have filled in this questionnaire will know roughly where they stand in relationship to others of the same sex. This particular sex difference is very important in understanding the degree to which men and women are likely to achieve marital satisfaction and happiness, because a person's score is governed in part by genetic factors.

Nature and nurture
Today the argument about sex differences is largely between environmentalists and hereditarians. Environmentalists ex-

149

plain the differences as the result of social and economic pressures, while hereditarians argue that heredity plays some part in shaping and maintaining these differences. This debate is often referred to as 'nature versus nurture': hereditarians say that sex differences are born (nature) rather than made (nurture), while the environmentalists argue the opposite. In this chapter I will look at the evidence for and against the nurture side of the argument. In the next chapter I will deal with some very interesting biological evidence that supports the case for heredity.

Blue for a boy, pink for a girl

Social tradition, transmitted through parents, is a popular explanation for the creation of sex differences. Parents, say environmentalists, sex-type their children from the moment of birth. In one study, parents were asked to describe their one-day-old infants as they would to a relative or close friend. It turned out that boy and girl babies, identical in birth-weight, length and various other medical indices, were indeed subject to parental prejudice. Female infants were more frequently described as 'little', 'beautiful', 'cute', 'delicate', 'like her mother' and so on, while newborn males were perceived as firmer, larger-featured, better-coordinated, more alert, stronger and hardier!

Another experiment presented some mothers with a six-month-old boy, dressed in blue and referred to as 'Adam'. Later, the same infant, now in a pink dress, was shown to the same mothers under the guise of 'Beth'. The mothers held the child and played with him/her for several minutes: they handed a doll more frequently to 'Beth', and a train more frequently to 'Adam', where both were equally available. They also smiled at the infant more often when they thought it was a female. Taped sessions have shown that fathers give sons more attention than daughters, while mothers show the opposite effect.

Kindergarten and school

It's clear, then, that there are many pressures on children to behave as society expects boy-children and girl-children to behave. By the kindergarten stage, girls are more likely than their male counterparts to paint, help the teacher, look at books or listen to stories, whereas little boys prefer to hammer and play with trucks, cars and guns. Generally speaking, boys play with 'masculine' toys, while girls prefer softer toys and dolls. These differences in behaviour seem to continue on past kindergarten into early youth, where we find boys preferring games involving physical strength, body contact, competition and toughness, while girls stick to activities requiring verbal

151

activity and singing, and those calling for a cooperative taking of turns. But are these role-playings inherent or merely *encouraged*? Perhaps boys play with trucks because they are given trucks. As Professor Wesley of Portland State University has put it:

> From childhood we are taught what to do and what not to do, and in addition to these teachings, we model that which we see around us. Thus, our language and thoughts and much of our likes and dislikes, and, of course, our sex-role stereotypes become established through learning in one way or another . . . Sex roles are learned perhaps in a cumulative fashion during all phases of our development.

The 'model' child

Such gender-oriented role-playing is so strongly reinforced in our daily lives that many people believe we become like Pavlov's dogs, eventually responding automatically in masculine or feminine ways as we are rewarded for doing so. This is sometimes called 'modelling', and it is another way in which society interjects its rigid rules; from infancy on, parents, teachers, and playmates alike encourage us with rewards, as well as with negative discouraging responses, to act in the manner 'appropriate' to our particular gender. Our social heritage appears to be as strong an influence as our genetic inheritance.

Is biology destiny?

There are so many social pressures that shape our behaviour from birth that anyone who would argue for a purely genetic interpretation of sex differences would clearly be going against the facts.

But it is possible to maintain a different theory: that there are biological differences between the sexes which affect their behaviour in important ways – and which have proved useful throughout evolution. This theory suggests that it was the

biological differences which caused the development of the sexual stereotypes we still follow.

If nature and nurture are so closely intertwined and interdependent, how can we hope to disentangle them for long enough to see if one is more important than the other?

There are two ways in which we can study the relationship between genetic and environmental factors in determining gender behaviour. The first approach is *biological*, and it involves working with theories about the effects of male and female hormones on both human and animal behavioural patterns. This approach will be studied in Chapter 7. The second approach, which might be called the *anthropological* or *sociological* way of looking at things, has itself various possibilities for study. One way is to study the *universality of certain sex differences*.

If a particular form of sex-related behaviour seems to be found in all types of societies, it could hardly be without any

153

biological basis. An alternative method requires an investigation into human societies or groups in which different kinds of behaviour models were offered or encouraged. Certain experimental organizations, for example the Israeli kibbutz movement, have insisted upon relationships antithetical to traditional gender role-playing. If social pressure is the determining factor in sex stereotyping, then such societies should develop young men and women behaviourally different from the traditional norms. If the influence of genetic factors is the stronger point, however, then male and female role-playing should survive such regimes.

Unfair advantage

Before examining either the sociological or biological approach, however, let's look at one extremely important factor that determines gender role-playing. That factor is *simple physical strength*. No generation has ignored it in its historical or political sense when referring to mankind in general; it is when psychologists have more recently had to deal with the topic of *womankind* that we have seen a tremendous reluctance to draw attention to one clear, cruel example of *innate inequality between the sexes*. Quite bluntly, men are physically stronger than women.

The importance and power of male strength has always been recognized, whether in individual situations or in political or historical contexts. Stronger, taller, more muscular boys nearly always come to lord it over their weaker counterparts, establishing patterns of dominance-submission; self-confidence versus uncertainty; feelings of superiority as opposed to those of inferiority. What works for boys in the classroom exists among adult males in the workplace, a process particularly obvious within the working classes. And even though intelligence and training and other personality factors play an important part in power struggles within the middle and upper classes, this 'strength factor' still holds weight. And *height*, too, as a matter of fact: recent studies have shown that tall men average 10 per cent higher earnings than their shorter counterparts.

The darker side of strength
Unfortunately, it is all too painfully clear that strength not only decides who can use power, but who can *abuse* it as well. Why do men rape women? *Because they can.* Sheer brute strength enables them to do so. Why do we have wife-beating rather than husband-beating? Because men have the muscles to do it. Studies have shown that more than half of America's wives are victims of physical abuse by their spouses, and at least 10 per cent of these unfortunate women have suffered from *extreme* violence, with broken limbs and hospital treatment a common experience. And, lest anyone think that this is a cultural factor, Drs Russell and Rebecca Dobash from Stirling University in Scotland have conducted studies which clearly show that wife abuse in Great Britain is as endemic as in the United States. They also assure us that 'A frequent and brutal use of force against wives by their husbands can be found among all classes: the middle class has the facilities to disguise it better and the beatings may be less audible to the neighbours.'

To have and hold . . . against her will
A newly discussed, if long-practised, form of wife abuse is increasingly apparent in magazines, books and newspapers these days, and that is *marital rape*. Again, men are simply strong enough to have intercourse with their wives whether the latter wish to or not . . . and they are doing so at an alarming rate. One German study demonstrated that fully 20 per cent of all married women had at one time or another been forced to endure sexual intercourse, the 'choice' often being that or a beating. And, until recently, and going back as far as Biblical times, there has been absolutely nothing illegal about this brutal, coercive practice! The laws are changing in some states in the USA and in various other nations as well, but this

commonly legally and even morally accepted practice is otherwise a perfect example of a social custom growing out of a biological necessity. Men could beat and rape their women because they were strong enough to do so, and they legitimized such actions in their mores and lawbooks.

Ignoring the obvious

Why are people, and this includes men as well as women, reluctant to bring up this issue of physical strength? Why are they hesitant to discuss the social ramifications of this fact when the examples are so obvious, and indeed universal throughout human history? Probably because they are *painful* as well. Primarily, however, this painful reality is ignored because it is so blatantly and biologically *unfair*. Yet, even in our allegedly advanced society, physical strength allied to cruelty and inhumanity can still be a very important factor. As we have seen, the physical abuse of women by men continues, with the law an almost impotent spectator. Because these facts are

extremely undesirable, and because we would rather things were different, we tend to overlook the extent to which a biological factor – superior male strength – creates a social structure favouring men over women.

This does not mean, of course, that we should not continue to try to legislate fairness and equality; it simply means that we must recognize what we are up against in our own biological heritage. Perhaps it was there in our evolutionary ancestors. Certainly, we see in primates, such as chimpanzees, dominant male behaviour based on aggression, and female behaviour characterized by submissiveness and appeasement. Women's liberationists may abhor traditional female stratagems of deceit and seduction, but they should also accept their possible inherent, biological origin.

Patriarchy: a biological burden?

There is at least one universal human institution which may lay claim to having roots in biological sex differences. That is patriarchy, defined by Professor Stephen Goldberg, author of *The Inevitability of Patriarchy*, as 'any system or organization (political, economic, industrial, financial, religious or social) in which the overwhelming number of upper positions in hierarchies are occupied by males'. We see it among lions, baboons, and the majority of other mammals which live in groups. There, the normal pattern is domination by a young strong male surrounded by a harem of females and their young. Normally the pattern is of weaker young males being driven out of the group by the dominant, strong male, who in turn will grow old and eventually be subdued or even killed by a new more youthful male. Human societies, too, see the rise and fall of leaders. The process of displacing them is more usually a matter of politics than of physical combat. But, in the past, physical strength was a quality to be valued in a human leader, and it is likely that male-dominated human hierarchies grew out of patterns of dominance originally based on the superior strength of the male.

Patriarchy is universal

As Professor Goldberg has stated, 'There is not, nor has there ever been, any society that even remotely failed to associate authority and leadership in superfamilial areas with the male.' His studies have exposed the myths and legends about matriarchies: he has shown that they are popular, albeit

imaginary, stories. Even the equality publicized in the more advanced modern societies, is more often than not more propaganda than practised policy. Golda Meir, Indira Gandhi, Margaret Thatcher may be more the exceptions to the rule than the proof of modern advancement.

The lie of socialist equality

Radical, so-called egalitarian, non-sexist socialist societies, from Cuba to Sweden, are no less hypocritical in their 'fair' treatment of women. In Communist China, for example, publicly committed to equalization since the Revolution, female equality is no more than window dressing. At the time Goldberg conducted his research, 13 of the 14 leaders of the Standing Committee of the National People's Congress, all 17 members of the State Council, and all 67 heads of the General Ministers were men.

The USSR is hardly less sexist than its Oriental neighbour. In the Soviet Union, where even the theories of biology taught in the educational system deny the relevance of biology to human behaviour, 96.9 per cent of all the members of the Central Committee were male at the time of Goldberg's studies.

A cook is not a chef

Margaret Mead, one of the world's foremost anthropologists, has stated, in her review of Goldberg's work, that 'Men have always been the leaders in public affairs and the final authorities at home.' This is true in both the psychological and practical aspects of human society. As for the former, Goldberg has gone on to say the following:

> The male strength and dominance and the female gentleness and endurance portrayed in our novels and movies mirror not merely *our* society's view of the emotional natures of men and women, but the views of every society that has ever existed.

159

And, so far as social practice is concerned, Goldberg also states that 'Every society gives higher status to male roles than to the non-maternal roles of females.' Indeed, in every society, males tend to attain the high-status (non-maternal) roles and positions and perform the high-status tasks, whatever those tasks are. In other words, not only do men get the better jobs: if a man is doing it, it *becomes* a better job. In Russia, for instance, where the majority of doctors are females, the medical vocation commands much less status and reward than it does in the West. And in America and most European nations, the 'little woman' may be the cook at home, but it is the male who is the paid and respected chef. This was once true of designers as well: men created 'fashion', while women did 'sewing'. Fortunately, things do seem to be changing and opening up for women. The question is, of course, how much change can be hoped for in a basically, biologically patriarchal society?

The kibbutz experiment

To what extent can our innate and biologically determined tendencies be altered by changing the roles that men and women play in a society? How important is the effect that can result from changing the teaching and the example that the young receive from their elders? More specifically, what would happen in a society that explicitly expressed the importance of absolute equality of men and women? What would happen if men and women were encouraged to do the same kind and amount of work; if outside caretakers tended to the children, and thus freed the women from traditional responsibilities; if the children themselves were brought up together in an egalitarianism which completely obliterated gender role stereotypes? Finally, what would happen if the family unit was itself destroyed in order to remove all traces of sex-role conditioning? Experiments such as these actually took place several decades ago in what is now Israel. There, Jewish settlers founded a type of farming commune known as a kibbutz. In the kibbutzim, all was ordered along the lines of total equality between the sexes. Work was shared equally, there was no distinction in dress, and cohabitation was actively discouraged. Children were brought up communally, away from their parents, and every effort was made to see that boys and girls were treated identically.

These dedicated communities make a useful test case for the effects of social pressures on traditional sex roles. Did the kibbutz experiment have any lasting effect on those who grew up under the kibbutz regime? In an important research project, the American anthropologist Melford E. Spiro studied the Kiryat Yedidim kibbutz in Israel for 30 years, from its foundation to the present day, and his findings are astonishing, to say the least. They have much to say about the influence of society and the value of indoctrination, some of it not very pleasing to the ears of modern-day feminists.

In the early years of the kibbutz the men and women worked side by side in the fields in accordance with basic kibbutz philosophy. Everyone did the same amount and kind of work. However, the experiment reaped something decidedly different from what it attempted to sow. The women found it too difficult working with the heavy tractors, and indeed such work was held responsible for the high incidence of miscarriages. So the workload was changed, and shortly thereafter there came a re-emergence of sexual specialization. Women took over the nursing, the nurseries, the school teaching, and child care. In time, the gender division of work was complete, with 88 per cent of the women involved in services, child care and education, and only 12 per cent working on the land. Indeed, the modern Sabra, or second-generation Israeli woman, regards farmwork as an undesirable option, quite unimbued with any sort of ideological egalitarian romance.

The early kibbutz attempted to do the same thing in government as it tried in education, and with similar results. Female kibbutz members were encouraged to take part in all political activity and to attend the General Assembly, the governing body. However, female participation became less and less frequent over the years. The Sabras were simply more interested in taking care of their families than in taking part in the political system.

The downgrading of marriage was another goal of early kibbutz life which saw a return to traditional ways as the young women grew up. During the first years of the kibbutzim marriages were legitimized merely for pragmatic purposes, and celebrations were considered scandalous – as was public marital affection. In the modern kibbutz marriage is considered important, and kibbutz budgeting is geared toward the couple rather than the group. Along these same lines, the once permissive practice of divorce is now frowned upon, and the divorce rate is very low; similarly, extramarital affairs are out and fidelity is in! And, in parallel with traditional marriage values, most Sabra men rate work as their most important activity, whereas the Sabra women grant the family and the home the same consideration.

Femininity in general was disregarded by the early kibbutz pioneers. Men and women were encouraged to dress alike, and sexual dimorphism was highly discouraged. Today, however, not only do Sabra women dress in traditional feminine fashion, but clothes in general, together with jewellery and cosmetics, are important consumer items for the Sabra women. Indeed, many kibbutzim now boast their own beauty parlours!

How did these changes come about? Why did joint showers for boys and girls, the discouragement of the nuclear family as a medium for child-rearing, the allocation of equal play and work for both sexes, and non-sexist education in the schools result in Sabra women who displayed a greater leaning to traditional ways and values over the years than their female counterparts living outside the kibbutzim in Israel? The answer is unclear, but it does lead to a new question: can we ever dismiss the importance and impact of our genetic inheritance? Chapter 7 will explore this issue more fully.

7

The biology of sex differences

In the last chapter we cited enough evidence to make the point about the strong possibility of innate differences between the sexes in their social and sexual behaviour. The actual differences found in most Western cultures seem to be universal, and this offers a strong, if unpopular, argument for the belief that biological factors are at the root of gender distinctions.

Dominance versus domesticity
These differences between the sexes are found across the globe. Everywhere, men appear to be more dominant, women more domestic. Studies show that, all over the world, males, more than women, enjoy impersonal and permissive sex; whether in Japan or in America, anthropological research has revealed that men display greater sexual promiscuity, more pleasure-seeking attitudes, fewer inhibitions, more interest in illicit sexual practices, and show less disgust at bizarre erotic pastimes than women do. And this difference is reflected in males' more favourable attitudes towards nudity, voyeurism, prostitution and pornography.

Past and present
The French have a timeless and truthful saying: 'The more things change, the more they remain the same.' Differences between the sexes are not only consistent across the globe but have always been so. Throughout recorded history, artists and poets have been commenting on what makes a man different

from a woman, and the same distinctions keep appearing over and over again. Read this comment in ancient Greece's bawdy playwright Aristophanes' *Thesmaphoriazusae*, and judge for yourself the extent to which it still applies today:

> Pray, why do you like us to be at home, all ready to smile and greet you / And storm and sulk if your poor little wife isn't always there to meet you?

It is important to understand what these gender-identified differences really mean, because there has been much confusion in recent history. For example, Kinsey reported incorrectly when he said that women are generally less stimulated than men by erotica. Disgust does not necessarily indicate a lack of interest. In studies where men and women have been shown explicit sexual films in laboratory conditions, they have been equally aroused by the testing stimuli. This can be seen not only by their answers to questionnaires; it has also been scientifically observed by direct measurement of penile erection and vaginal lubrication. By the same token, it is invalid to suggest that women respond more to 'romantic' love scenes, and men to explicitly sexual ones. The physiological and psychological responses are the same; it is the *evaluation* that makes the difference. Arousal simply doesn't mean enjoyment *per se*, for many women are disgusted despite their body changes, and refuse to see them through. Sometimes arousal causes only guilt, or fear of the sexual stimulation as a threat.

The intra-sexual difference

In this chapter, I am going to review evidence which suggests that sex hormones are responsible for the differences which have been observed between male and female behaviours. But before I do so, we should remember that the differences within each sex are greater than the differences between the sexes, even on such a score as that of our libido scale. The difference

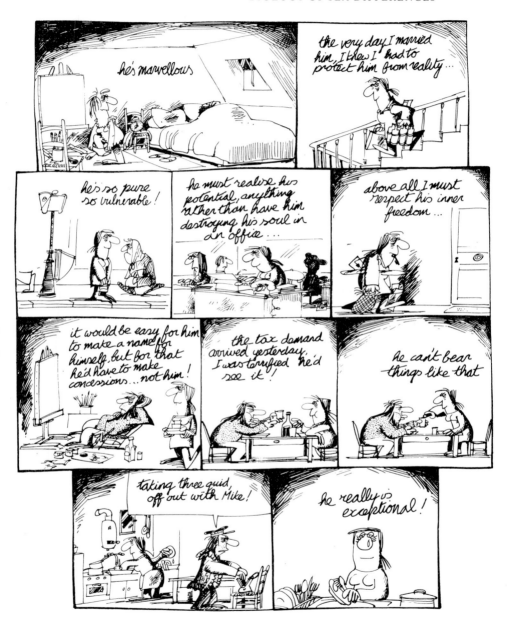

there between males and females is about 7 points; but the difference between the highest and the lowest scoring males is 27, and that between the highest and lowest scoring females is 26! It may be, then, that differences within each sex can also be explained in terms of hormones. This argument would fit well with the fact that genetic influences are very important in determining a person's score on the libido scale.

A difference of conception

Whenever we discuss the biological basis of maleness and femaleness, it is crucial to remember that there are *two* specific periods involved in the determination of any individual's sexual and social behaviour. The first, of course, is the moment of conception itself: the nature of the sex chromosome is determined at the instant of fertilization, when the sperm and ovum are united. If the resulting foetus combines two X chromosomes it will become a biological female; if there is a combination of an X with the male Y chromosome, then we have a biological male. This, however, is only half the issue.

The role of the brain

It appears that the second half of our genetic sexual identity is formed just before we leave the womb. Immediately before birth there are sex hormones circulating in the blood of the foetus that produce anatomical differences between the male and female brain, and result in different patterns of connections between the nerve cells. This 'cerebral masculinization' takes place only during this brief, critical period, and once the pattern has been established *there is no way of changing it*. One should always keep in mind, however, that this 'masculiniza-tion' is only a matter of sexual and social behavioural difference; abilities such as intelligence and logical thinking do not become the exclusive property of a 'masculine' or 'feminine' brain.

Experimental work regarding these chromosomal sex differences in human beings is rightly prohibited in any civilized society. However, certain accidents of nature, along with misunderstood medical treatments, have inadvertently tested these theories. Active research on 'brain masculinization', of course, is left to work with animals.

The laboratory evidence

The manipulation of hormones in various rodents has clearly demonstrated gender differences at least in the animal world. When research scientists have castrated male rats or injected womb-bound female rodents with androgens (male hormones), physical and behavioural changes have taken place. Genetic females produced male genitalia along with their own ovaries, and the opposite occurred with the genetic males. The new ways the rats behaved, however, was even more intriguing than their altered bodies. When physically normal female rats were exposed to androgens immediately following their birth they exhibited typical male behaviour, including fighting, struggling for dominance, and attempting to mount other females! Their male rodent counterparts demonstrated feminine patterns of behaviour when they were castrated immediately after being born. However, even more interesting than these dramatic results, was another startling conclusion drawn during the experimentation. The existence and importance of a *critical time period* was easily demonstrated by the fact that identical hormonal experiments carried out either earlier or later in reference to the birth resulted in *no* observable behaviour changes whatsoever! It was crucial that the experiment should take place at exactly the right moment.

Structural differences

There is strong evidence, too, that sex hormones affect the actual brain structure of rats. The size of various cell clusters in a part of the brain called the hypothalamus has been shown to differ according to the animal's gender. The pattern of connections between the cells also varies according to whether the rat is male or female.

The influence of sex hormones on the mammalian brain decreases in animals higher up the evolutionary ladder, but some effects still remain. It is a big step from rat to monkey, but scientists have seen androgen-induced dominance behaviour in female apes as well as submissive patterns resulting from castration in male members of the species. This works even in regard to very specific behaviour. Rhesus monkeys, for instance, have very particular mounting procedures, starting with both feet on the ground and then using their feet to climb upon the female as mating progresses. Female monkeys never indulge in this sort of behaviour, but foetally masculinized females will invariably try this method of mating.

The hormonal factor: accident and design

We spoke earlier of 'brain masculinization' being inadvertently proven either through the mistake of man or nature. One unfortunate, if revealing, case involved disastrous side effects produced when hormones were given to prevent miscarriage.

The hormones in question belonged to a group of steroids, first synthesized in the 1950s, which were related in chemical structure to androgens but were in biological action simply substitutes for the pregnancy hormone called progesterone. Hence the drugs were called *progestines*.

Unbeknown to the doctors using them at the time, these anti-miscarriage progestines exerted, under certain circumstances, a masculinizing influence, first on the female foetus, and then on the female infants themselves. Extreme results produced girl babies actually born with a penis. Doctors assumed these genetic females to be boys born with undescended testicles, and the children were brought up as males. Other genetic females were less dramatically masculinized, requiring only surgical adjustment of their external genitalia. They were brought up as girls, the onset of puberty adjusting the body physically with menstruation and general feminizing.

There is a *genetic* defect comparable to this unfortunate consequence of scientific research, and it is called the *adreno-genital syndrome.* This defines an abnormality of development in which the adrenal glands are prevented from synthesizing the proper hormone (called cortisone), releasing instead androgens which masculinize the foetus by entering its bloodstream. When physicians establish this diagnosis in the newborn infant girl, minor vaginal surgery is sometimes

'I understand she's something in biology.'

required to start the child's feminine growth. In addition, and more importantly, hormones are regulated from birth onwards by treatment with cortisone, which stems further postnatal masculinization.

In other words, in order to fight the masculinization effects created by the release of these male hormones during the critical pre-birth period, little girls are treated anatomically, medicinally, and even socio-psychologically as they are reared in feminine fashion. Is this sufficient to make the behaviour of these girls traditionally feminine? The answer would appear to be *no*.

Girls may be boys . . .

Investigators compared the behaviour of these genetically 'masculinized' females with a control group of normal girls matched on the basis of age, intelligence, socio, economic background, and also race. Their conclusions were startling. Even when the control-group girls were blood relatives of the masculinized females, the differences were notable. The masculinized girls were more likely to regard themselves as tomboys, whether created by nature or man's error. Nine of the 10 girls with the progestine-induced syndrome and 11 of the 13 of those suffering from the adreno-genital syndrome claimed they were tomboys, an opinion heartily agreed upon by their mothers, playmates and peers. In addition, the masculinized girls also expressed a desire to have been born a male; or at the least they were ambivalent on the subject. The control girls had no such wish.

The masculinized girls also exhibited a high level of physical energy expenditure, indulging in vigorous outdoor play, games and sports more generally associated with boys. It is interesting to note here that in this one respect these girls resembled the prenatally masculinized Rhesus females, who also participated in typically masculine rough-and-tumble play. Team games such as baseball and football were favourites of these masculinized girls, and many preferred to have boys as

playmates. The American professor J. Money, the person most closely associated with these studies, has made the following comment:

> Dominance, assertion and striving for position in the dominance hierarchy of childhood is a variable most characteristic of the masculinized girls, as compared with the others.

Dressing the part

There were also differences between the control girls and their masculinized counterparts in relation to clothing and other adornment. The masculinized girls seemed to prefer utilitarian or functional clothing, the others wanting chic, pretty or fashionable 'feminine' garb. The masculinized girls wanted to wear slacks and shorts, the control group again preferring more traditional female articles such as dresses and skirts. One cannot help but compare these subjects to Spiro's kibbutzim Sabras who also chose 'feminine' dress along with jewellery and makeup and hairstyling. It may well be, then, that an apparently free choice – to dress in one way or another – is influenced by biological factors.

Toying with sex

The masculinized girls also preferred those toys usually given to boys, showing an indifference to or blatant neglect of dolls and similarly feminine toys. And, unlike the control group girls, these masculinized young females extended this lack of interest in dolls to actual infants themselves, refusing to play with them and expressing no interest in babysitting for their infant brothers or sisters. They stated either that they would not have children or that they would treat them in a matter-of-fact, perfunctory manner. And, in relation to this, masculinized girls also expressed a clear preference for career rather than marriage should they have to make the choice.

Boys will be . . . girls

Complementary to the studies of the adreno-genital syndrome and progestine-induced hermaphroditism is another genetically-induced phenomenon called the *androgen-insensitivity syndrome*. In this case a baby is born a genetic male in that he possesses the XY chromosome and not the XX chromosomal characteristics of the female. However, he is also born with apparently normal external female genitalia. And, during puberty, there is enough of the female hormone called estrogen produced for the female secondary sexual characteristics to develop.

This disease is caused at the basic hormonal level, and continues from foetal life onwards. The pre-born baby and subsequent infant simply cannot use the normal amounts of the male testerone that the body produces, but it still responds to the female estrogens created in the testes. The result, unfortunately, is an imbalance in hormones that ultimately causes a failure in the pre-natal masculinizing process in the brain. The effect on these genetic males is a mix-up in gender behaviour development: not only does the masculinization of these children not occur, a feminization takes place that continues throughout the child's development.

These genetic boys do not grow up to be boys as we know them. The male victims of this birth defect acted in many ways like little girls. Later, as they reached maturity, they behaved as young women. Eight out of 10 of these feminized boys preferred to play with dolls and other toys, and their actual playtime was taken up by the less rugged activities. In later years *none* reported that a career was more important than marriage, and not one was involved in a career during the duration of the study. Professor June Reinisch of Columbia University Teachers' College made a thorough review of all the evidence and summed it up in the following way:

It follows, from the evidence presented on the clinical syndromes, that foetal androgens probably do affect the human brain in a similar manner to that demonstrated in rodents and lower primates. That is, the presence of androgen during the critical period in pre-natal development mediates organization and differentiation in the central nervous system in both genetic males and females so that male patterns of response and sensitivity in later life to 'male' sex hormones are augmented and insensitivity to 'female' hormones and suppression of female patterns are produced . . . Conversely, the hypothesis proposed by the experimenters with animals was substantiated, that the absence of androgens . . . influences the development of female external genital morphology [and results] in feminine patterns and preferences. More specifically, the data suggest that the absence or presence of androgens *in utero* may be involved in the organization and differentiation of certain patterns of human cognition and intellectual functioning and energy expenditure, and influence the acquisition of other sexually dimorphic behaviours and interests found in humans. . . The effect of foetal androgen on the central nervous system has been demonstrated to continue to exert its influence into adulthood, in both animals and humans, thereby suggesting that the modification, organization and differentiation which might occur in its presence during the critical period are permanent.

Do exceptions prove the rule?

There is evidence, then, that biological changes at the foetal stage can influence children's behaviour. If the normal hormonal changes do not take place, genetically male children may behave in ways more usually associated with females and vice versa, despite the pressures to conform to the male or female stereotype.

More evidence to support this view comes from the Dominican Republic in the Caribbean. Here it is relatively common for genetically male infants to be born with female physical characteristics. This condition, rare in other parts of the world, is believed to be due to inbreeding and other genetic accidents. Brought up from birth as girls, the people concerned find that as puberty approaches their voices deepen and they develop male genitals and male-type musculature. They begin to take an interest in girls, generally adopt male roles, and frequently go on to marry and become fathers! Despite being reared as girls, they often begin to think of themselves as boys at the age of five or six. In other words, the masculinized brains of such children take precedence over the physical development even in such extreme cases.

Sex differences and sociobiology

In considering the pros and cons of nature versus nurture so far two main points have emerged. The first is that at all times and in all societies male behaviour has tended to be more aggressive and dominating than female behaviour. The second is that, whatever the power of social conditioning, biological factors have a far-reaching effect in the development of differences between male and female behaviour. To which we should add a third point, that the general differences observed between the sexes is only generally true: in at least one measure, as we have seen, the degree of individual difference within each sex is far greater than the general difference between them. I'll be returning to the question of individual differences later in this chapter.

177

Is there a theory which explains how these differences were useful to the human species in the first place, and why they have been maintained over so long? Can we, in short, account for the differences in social and sexual attitudes between men and women? One group of researchers, the sociobiologists, have tried to explain the typical behaviour patterns seen in our society in terms of Darwinian evolution.

They point to the general differences in sexual behaviour between men and women that we have already noted. Men tend to be more promiscuous than women, with a higher libido and a greater interest in unusual sexual activities or perversions. Women, on the other hand, tend to have fewer sexual partners, and a lower interest in unusual or perverted sexual activity. Moreover, men are more attracted by physical attributes, women more attracted by intelligence, personality and status.

The environmentalist, or nurture, argument explains this as the result of strong sexual taboos on female promiscuity by a male-dominated society. But a study which compared the sexual behaviour of homosexual men with that of homosexual women showed a considerable difference in libido. Presumably, homosexual relationships are to some extent free of the rules imposed by society on heterosexual behaviour. There is no risk, for example, of an unwanted pregnancy. Yet, while homosexual males find partners at a rate between 10 and 100 times that of heterosexual men, lesbian relationships are neither shorter nor longer than those of heterosexual women.

The sociobiologist theories, which have a great deal of relevance to sexual relationships in general, and more specifically to our topic of marriage, explain these differences in the following ways.

Sexual evolution
Darwin pointed out that nature is geared to the survival of those mutations which best fit the environment. The sociobiologists have taken this idea one step further to suggest

that what is really crucial is the individual's fitness in relation to his ability to have descendants, to transmit his own genes to later generations to ensure the perpetuation of his species. Taking this point of view, our bodies and brains are mere instruments in the vast evolutionary process, transient machines geared to the preservation or proliferation of our genes. Through millions of years our physical selves and our social behaviour have been shaped and strengthened in order that we may survive through our own progeny.

Keeping this basic idea in mind, the innate differences in reproductive strategies of men and women are quite extraordinary. The male reproductive system is capable of supplying millions of sperms over an exceedingly long period of time. A single male's orgasms ultimately produce over 100 000 000 sperms in a lifetime! Women, on the other hand, have only a limited supply of eggs; they can only have the egg fertilized once a month; these eggs deteriorate over a period of time and, eventually, the menopause stops their production altogether. What is the point of all this? How, according to sociobiologists, do these startling differences between the male and female animal work for the evolutionary advantage of humankind?

Sociobiologists suggest that, in order to ensure the preservation of their genetic material, 'men'-kind have evolved over the last three million years a strategy quite different from the methods of 'women'-kind. They argue that there is a biological instinct at work that urges males to distribute their genetic material, their sperms, as far and as wide as possible, thus attempting to impregnate as many women as possible. This genetic drive is, of course, 'seminal' as regards the issue of male promiscuity (although it would seem to be quite counterproductive in this age of overpopulation). The female instinct, on the other hand, is to be choosy, selective of the sperm which will fertilize the small number of eggs she will produce in her lifetime.

From this viewpoint, the considerable length of female human gestation, a full nine months, also contributes to

179

woman's biological choosiness. She is unable to conceive
during this time, and that makes her all the more meticulous
about the quality of sperm, of the very life which she will carry
on for her species. Among lower species, this biological
difference between males and females often results in indiscri-
minate behaviour on the part of the male animal – there are
recorded cases of male frogs attempting to mate with galoshes,
and of male butterflies trying to couple with leaves! Females of
these species, however, *never* make such mistakes, nor may it be
natural for human females to mate with any male who comes
along. This conflict may be amusing in the case of other
animals, but it is the basis of the battle between the sexes
among *Homo sapiens*.

Jealousy: a male prerogative?

Jealousy is another characteristic more common to men than
women: this may have to do with the potential problem of
deception over fatherhood. 'A wise mother knows her own

child'; a man can never be that certain about his child's paternity. This dichotomy helps explain the natural male possessiveness, one of the more troublesome aspects of the double standard. It is in his biological interest to keep his woman away from temptation in order to ensure that he is the natural father of his children.

Among wild animals a group of females under the domination of a single male is an extreme example of this general tendency towards paternity preservation. The male animal not only wants to mate with as many females as he possibly can; he wishes to make sure that he is the *only* one to do so. And it is a fact that we see the harem not only throughout the animal kingdom but also in human history. In the wild, invasion by another male is often the cue for aggressive behaviour by the dominant male; in the human world, too, male interlopers in the harem have risked death or disfigurement.

Attraction will be opposite
These basic biological differences between men and women, the former's predilection for seduction and the latter's preference for careful selection, tend also to explain the differences in the male and the female's idea of what is attractive in the male sex. Dr Glenn Wilson, a noted British expert in the field of human sexual behaviour, has said the following:

> Men are typically seeking what they describe as physically attractive women, by which they mean indications of fertile ground in which to plant their seed. The woman should be young (so her eggs have not gone bad), she should have clear eyes and an unblemished complexion (indicating health). She is more desirable with proportionately large breasts and hips (the better to bear children), and of course, a narrow waist is also attractive because this signifies that she is not already pregnant (no sense in wasting time and

181

semen if she is). Women are seeking evidence that a man is superior breeding material, which means physical strength and skills relevant to defence and provision. Since the evolutionary history of *Homo sapiens* is parallel with the shift of emphasis from brute strength to intelligence, most women today are more impressed with the latter. To some extent, each sex shares the interest of the other, for there are also evolutionary limits set on the degree of divergences between the sexes, but for the moment we are concerned with differences rather than similarities.

All of this, of course, is subject to changing mores and values, and the individual man and woman will also have his or her own preferences. An intelligent man is any sensible woman's goal for a relationship, but it is the tough, good-looking heroes, rather than eggheads, that draw the high ratings on television. Still, you may like to try this little test on yourself and your friends. A friend offers to arrange a blind date. What is the first question you ask him/her about this potential romantic companion? Nine times out of ten, women will ask 'What does he do?'; whereas men will want to know 'What does she look like?'. There is no scientific validity to this test, but it is important to remember what is common in human behaviour, and this may come from our biological inheritance.

Sexual preferences

There is a further outstanding difference between men and women that cannot be accounted for by sex-role learning. It also seems to be immune to elimination or change by social conditioning. Keep in mind that history has not presented us with a *Marquise* de Sade . . . This is the matter of the propensity toward perversity, proneness to sexual deviation always being more characteristic of men than women. Wilson has also pointed out that whether fetishists, transvestites, exhibitionists, voyeurs, sadomasochists, necrophiliacs, frotteurs, transsexuals, all are far more likely to be men than women. Female paedophilia is rare, and even homosexual men outnumber lesbians to a considerable degree. So far as it is possible to judge, this appears to be true throughout recorded history. Wilson explains it in the following way, based upon his assumption that the male sex drive, unlike the feminine passive perceptiveness, is an active imperative:

> Males seek and approach objects in the environment that they find sexually exciting and the reception they get (whether rewarding or punishing) determines their subsequent interest in the object. The strongest biological impetus is toward adult females, but if these are sufficiently punishing or threatening the man may fall back on substitutes such as children, animals, corpses, or articles of female clothing. This is particularly likely to be the case when development towards maturity has been stunted in some way, e.g. by punitive and puritanical parents, or when the social skills required for seduction are not required for any reason.

> The same thing does not happen to women because their role is one of passive acceptance or rejection of the approaches of various men. If they had a bad experience with some particular man it usually doesn't matter much because it is cancelled out by the characteristics of subsequent suitors. Since women are seldom pursued by male boots or underwear, rubber blow-ups, sheep, children, or corpses, they do not often settle upon them as sources of sexual satisfaction. They sometimes receive overtures from lesbians, young men, alsatian dogs, and members of the immediate family, with the result that homosexuality, paedophilia, bestiality and incest are not unknown in women. But even then, the continuing advances of men reduce the chances of a fixation occurring. The normal woman devotes much more attention to the characteristics of the various men who try to arouse her – especially their qualities as potential studs and husbands.

183

The reality of orgasm

Another area which reflects the basic differences between men and women has to with *orgasm*. Talk shows discuss it; books tell you how to get it; *everybody* seems to worry about it; and about the only thing everyone agrees upon is the unpleasant fact that, in general, women seem to have more difficulty in having orgasms than do men. Some women report *never* having reached climax, and most women experience occasional failures to achieve orgasm. This does not seem to be a common problem of men, unless they are impotent. The difficulty that some women find in reaching orgasm is a problem that many would like to solve; the real problem, however, seems to be in the disagreement as to the *cause*.

Here again the argument is between the social and the biological, feminists usually taking a stand in relation to the former. They will usually point to sex-role learning and male chauvinism as the basic causes of female 'failure' to achieve orgasm. According to such arguments, the severe standards of morality imposed upon women through the centuries have made them frigid; they have been taught that it is 'unladylike' to have an orgasm. Selfish and inconsiderate behaviour on the part of men has also been cited as a cause of sexual inhibition in women.

Are men to blame?

No one is going to argue that a clumsy male lover is likely to result in a satisfactory time in bed. Common sense tells us otherwise. However, studies proving that male clumsiness is a basic cause of female frigidity are simply not supported. When a study was made of husbands of both orgasmic and non-orgasmic women, few obvious differences were found in the men with respect to their personality, education, social background, or even their techniques in lovemaking. Nor is there any evidence whatsoever that rape and other traumatic sexual experiences are likely to result in permanent impairment of a woman's responsiveness. The male is simply not responsible for all female sexual difficulties; the problem, if there is one, is more likely to be within the female herself. Obviously some sexual problems can be solved by a sympathetic, loving partner, but it is really more likely to be a problem of nature, not nurture. This sad but probably true assumption is also supported by what we find – or, rather, do *not* find – in the animal kingdom.

Evidence suggests that female orgasms are rare in the animal world. The females in non-primate or lower primate species do not appear to have orgasms at all, and only in some apes have tests shown physiological, orgasmic changes similar to those found in human beings. And it is interesting to note that these responses have *only* been found in zoo animals: there is no evidence for orgasm in the wild. Obviously, then, female orgasm, unlike the ejaculative response of the male animal, is not essential to the perpetuation of the species, and is therefore a waste of energy as far as nature is concerned. It is very likely that female orgasm is a product of civilization. To which, perhaps, we can say, hurray for civilization!

Whatever the reason, it is important to acknowledge such differences between the sexes. Men and women *are* different, and the 'quality in equality' may very well *be* in our differences. Obviously society has played a role in reinforcing particular patterns of behaviour, but it is foolish as well as useless to fight our genetic inheritance. Furthermore, it is really an insult to women to insist that they adapt themselves to the male standards of behaviour, because that only implies that there is such a thing as female inferiority. What is inferior about tenderness and caring? Do we really want more aggression in this world? Might not the drive to nurture offer a better example than the drive for power?

The lesson of biology

I've included the section on sociobology as one possible explanation of why men and women behave as they do, and why these behaviours have developed in the way they have.

185

William James, the great American psychologist and philosopher, once woke up in the middle of the night, convinced that he had been vouchsafed the secret of the Universe. he promptly wrote it down and then went back to sleep again. When he woke up in the morning, he found that he had written the following doggerel:

> Hogamous, higamous
> Man is polygamous
> Higamous, hogamous
> Woman monogamous

He was very disappointed, but he need not have been. This may not be the secret of the Universe, but it seems to be a fair representation of reality – something seldom given to philosophers. Moreover, it is no accident, but is deeply rooted in the hormonal secretions that bathe us from early foetal life, and in our genetic inheritance. That our genes, in their struggle for survival, should have through countless generations pushed men and women in these directions is to tell us something important about our lives, our sexual behaviour and the difficulties we face in marriage. The doctrine of evolution is the basis of biology: psychology can be no exception to this rule.

The right to be different

We have already seen that the biggest differences we measure are not those between the sexes, but within them. The various tests and questionnaires included in this book are based on research which clearly shows that there is a tremendous variety among individual men and women, that most of us deviate from the 'norm' in one direction or another. Societies have tended to make rules based only upon the averages, so perhaps it will be a mark of increasing civilization to recognize the differences and merits of everyone within his or her gender.

Extremes of either side generally tend to be dangerous. The sexual liberation of the sixties became the sexual enslavement of the 1970s, with both men and women feeling inadequate,

186

indeed, sexually sick, if they didn't care to have sex with anybody any time and in any place. Celia Haddon has discussed this 'immoral imperative' in her book, *Limits of Sex*, in which she points out that the real rebels of today are actually the celibates, or at least those people who maintain the value of a long-lasting relationship with restriction of sexual behaviour to one partner. She goes even further to state other dangers that have cropped up with our distortion of sex, with the three powerful myths which have come to dominate our thinking. 'These myths are that sex is harmless fun, that it is good for people, and that it is natural,' she says. She points out that this kind of careless thinking, propagated by all the media and by well-meaning if foolish social workers, psychiatrists, counsellors and 'sex experts', completely ignores the darker side of sex. What about the anger and aggression that are also a part of sex? What are we to say about rape; is this just an example of extreme aggressiveness in sex? And, if sex is always good for you, why are there now more deaths from contraception methods in England than there are from childbirth itself? If sex is so good for people, if casual sex is a healthy norm, then why is VD reaching epidemic proportions? Why are certain sexually-transmitted diseases, such as genital herpes, becoming immune to antibiotics?

The 'benefit' of the sexual revolution may indeed turn out to be a poisoned chalice. There is nothing 'healthy' about a monogamous man worrying that his fidelity is a sign of a lack of virility, nor is there anything pleasant about the fact that millions of women today fake orgasms because they believe that they are actually sick if they don't experience them. Sexual skill has become a modern 'idol of the tribe', and we have all become its victims.

Freedom in variety

The truth – and the beauty – of human nature lies in its diversity. The famous philosopher Immanuel Kant seems never to have slept with a woman, yet Captain Cook recorded that King Lapetakaka II of Tonga considered it his duty to engage in intercourse 8 to 10 times a day, even at the age of 80! Some people, whether from professional or vocational choice – as in the case of certain religious communities – or else because of personal feeling, have never experienced sex. On the other hand, Catherine the Great declared that human beings needed sex at least six times a day, and was said to follow her own prescription. A certain Mademoiselle DuBois, who lived just before the French Revolution, made a catalogue of her lovers over a twenty-year period that eventually totalled 16,527 individuals. 'Liberation for all' was the battle cry of the late 1960s, but what point is there in a permissive society that doesn't permit people to be themselves? A nationwide study of teenagers in Great Britain found 54 per cent of them agreeing with the statement that 'sexual permissiveness in our society had been allowed to go too far'. Virtually, or possibly virtuously, 75 per cent of those interviewed felt that they were under too much pressure to have sex.

While it is certainly wrong to forbid sexual expression, as was done in our puritanical and Victorian pasts, it is likewise immoral to propagandize for promiscuity. Liberation in moderation is probably the best policy; if some women wish to remain home and raise families then they should be allowed to do so. Similarly men who practise fidelity should not be accused of lack of libido. Social theories may be revealing, but they should state the situation, not set the standard. And it is also the task of science to present the facts to individual men and women, and to leave them to decide what kind of behaviour best suits their particular, individual nature.

8

Can an ailing marriage be improved?

So, now that we've seen that marriage is clearly a vital factor in the happiness of most people, that some form of marriage has been universal throughout recorded history in all known human societies, and that there is little chance of marriage being replaced by anything else in the foreseeable future, we have to ask ourselves again why almost 50 per cent of marriages in the United States end in divorce. Something is very wrong. There must be some reason why so many people find so much conflict and dissatisfaction in their marriages that they choose to leave what should be the most stabilizing influence in their lives. Can anything that I've discussed about what psychologists know about marriage and happiness shed any light on the current marriage crisis?

Certainly a person's genetic predisposition plays a role in whether or not he or she is apt to be happy in marriage, but that's far from the whole story. The fact is that our genes push us in a certain direction, but they do not *determine* what we will actually do in a given situation. Obviously our education and socialization play a large part in determining our actual behaviour. Both heredity and environment influence us. We can't do much about the traits that we've inherited, but we can decide how to handle them in daily life. We can recognize what type of personality we've been born with and then we can work toward adjusting it to complement the personality of the one we love, so that happiness in marriage will be more than just a fantasy.

What I hope I've done in this book is help you understand

your own needs and personality so that you can better choose a mate whose needs and personality are compatible with yours. But if you've already chosen a marriage partner, and if things aren't going very well, take heart, there are steps you can take to repair the damage, steps that have been tried by many with great success.

Marital therapy: past and present

Marriage counselling, in one form or another, is very ancient. For centuries, priests and religious leaders offered advice to their followers whose marriages were ailing. More recently, psychologists and psychoanalysts have entered the field. In the past, the personal happiness of the spouse was considered less important than the preservation of the marriage and the upholding of the religious orthodoxy. But, as psychiatrists and marriage counsellors got into the act, personal happiness of the person who consulted them began to become the barometer. Personally, I feel that much of the advice traditionally offered by the psychoanalytic community has been coloured by

192

Freudian theories which were often overgeneralized and which have never been proven to be effective in solving the problems of the couples in question.

Much more effective, I feel, is the behavioural approach to marital difficulties, which is a relative newcomer to the field. Behavioural therapy differs from conventional therapy in certain fundamental ways. First of all it is based on a well established set of psychological theories which have found ample support in experimental studies, both with animals and humans. Secondly, this type of treatment emphasizes actual behaviour rather than complex theories and interpretations of the unconscious process. And, thirdly, behavioural marital therapy, like behavioural therapy for neurotic disorders, has insisted on proof of its effectiveness through quantified results. This does not mean that other kinds of therapy are not effective, or that behavioural therapy is flawless. Certainly, various types of therapy work for some people in some situations, and we have a lot more to learn about behavioural therapy. But, even though we have a long way to go with this fairly new science, it has already taught us a great deal, and I'd like to summarize some of these findings here.

Rewarding good behaviour

Behavioural marital therapy is essentially based on one very simple but important psychological fact: that behaviour which produces rewards will tend to be repeated, whereas behaviour which produces punishment will tend to be eliminated. Modern psychologists often replace the word 'reward' with 'positive reinforcement', because the latter term has certain technical implications which the former doesn't. For instance, positive reinforcement is usually administered right after the action it is intended to reinforce, whereas a reward may be given at any time. Experiments have shown that the longer the delay, the less effective the reward. Another difference is that the definition of reward is usually made by the person giving it. Often the giver is mistaken in his choice of reward so that what he gives the receiver may not be thought of as positive reinforcement at all. So, positive reinforcement has come to be defined in terms of its actual effects – does it, in fact, make the action which it follows more likely to be repeated? As we've defined it, positive reinforcement is that kind of reward that works.

When psychologists use the term 'negative reinforcement', they don't mean punishment, but rather the cessation of punishment, and the reinforcement provided by this cessation for the activity preceding it. For example, let's say a woman is married to a lawyer who, every time they have a dinner party, talks only about law. After the guests have left she gets furious at him for being so dull and insensitive as to bore all the women at the table with relentless professional chatter. If she were to stop complaining about his boring legal monologues and start praising him every time he discussed a novel he'd read, his children, or the day's headlines, that would be 'negative reinforcement' for talking about his broader interests. The wife would be negatively reinforcing this more lively, social behaviour in her husband by ceasing her criticism of the behaviour she doesn't like.

All animal trainers work along these same lines. Suppose a trainer wants to teach a dog to come to him when he whistles. Rather than punishing the dog for failing to respond correctly, the trainer rewards the dog with food and affection when he does come. This way the dog is more likely to come when he hears the whistle in the future.

Some people find all of this a little threatening. People are not animals, they say, and their behaviour should not be compared with that of animals. But to say that in some ways we behave like animals is not to say that we behave like animals in all ways. Social scientists are trying to find out to what extent laws derived from animal behavioural experiments are applicable to man. Clearly, there are some important differences, just as there are some important similarities.

One of the most dramatic applications of these principles

that I know of has been with certain children who, for some unknown reason, have an uncontrollable urge to bang their heads against walls, doors, or almost any hard object they find. Obviously, these children can hurt themselves severely, and this behaviour must be stopped. In the past, pediatricians have suggested that the child be tied in his chair. This had the effect of temporarily stopping the behaviour, but usually, when finally released, the child would bang his head against the wall with renewed enthusiasm. Some psychoanalysts have ex-

plained this kind of behaviour in terms of an unconscious need to attract the mother's attention. According to this view, if the mother pays more attention to the child, he will stop the behaviour. Not so. When these mothers were instructed to pick the child up and hug and kiss him whenever he acted this way, they found that the child tended to bang his head even more, since he loved the additional attention and wanted even more.

So what was the final solution to this terrifying problem? The answer is simple. Whenever a child started to bang his head on the wall, his mother was told to pick him up, with no show of emotion, take him to a separate room and lock him in it for ten minutes. This was called 'time out'. After ten minutes she was told to go back to the room and let the child out, again with no show of emotion, and to keep on with her normal activities. Should an hour or so pass without the child banging his head, his mother was asked to pick him up and play with him, generally rewarding him by these instances of positive reinforcement for his good behaviour. Almost without exception it worked. Within a few days most of the head-bangers were cured.

Give and take in marriage

How, then, can we apply this reinforcement of behaviour principle to marriage? It all has to do with 'equity' or fairness. The principle of equity states that you must please your spouse in order for him or her to return the compliment and please you. The more equal the two sets of pleasures are, the happier the marriage will be. This may sound calculated and unromantic. However, based on careful observations of countless marriages, it's been shown that in happy marriages the pleasures are fairly equal, whereas in unhappy marriages one spouse fails to produce sufficient positive reinforcement to satisfy the other, and to repay him or her for pleasures received. Sometimes, both partners are equally at fault.

This equity principle was first used in marital therapy by an American named R. B. Stuart, who called it the 'reciprocity principle'. It is, according to Stuart, based on two major assumptions. The first: that 'the exact pattern of interaction which takes place between spouses at any point in time is the most rewarding of all the available alternatives'. So, he says, 'when a husband consistently fails to leave his friends in order to spend time with his wife, it may be concluded that his friends offer greater relative rewards than his wife'. The second: that 'most married adults expect to enjoy reciprocal relations with their partners'. This means that each party has rights and duties, and each is expected to reinforce the other equitably. 'Whenever one partner to a reciprocal interaction unilaterally rewards the other, he does so with the confidence that he will be compensated in kind in the future. For example, if the husband agrees to entertain his wife's parents for a weekend, he does so with the expectation that his wife will accompany him on a weekend fishing trip at some time in the the future,' says Stuart.

According to Stuart, this reciprocity, or give-and-take, develops as a consequence of a healthy history of positive reinforcement. There is a lot of evidence that shows that people are more attracted to others, and will reinforce these others more, if, in turn, they have been previously reinforced by them. 'When disordered marriages are evaluated in the light of this reinforcement/attraction hypothesis, it is seen that each partner reinforces the other at a low rate and each is therefore relatively unattractive to and unreinforced by the other.' This observation leads to Stuart's third assumption, that: 'in order to modify an unsuccessful marital interaction, it is essential to develop the power of each partner to mediate rewards for the other'. So, if we can learn how to please our partner so that he or she will both be happier and also be more likely to please us, then we have a prescription for a happy marriage, and a method for improving an unhappy one.

When things go wrong
When two people fail to provide balanced mutual reinforcement (when the reward level is too low for one or both partners)

then one of two things can happen. Either one or both partners tries to *coerce* the other, or there will be a *withdrawal* from the union by one or both partners.

An example of coercion would be something like this. Let's say that a husband wants his wife to be more affectionate, more responsive in bed, but he doesn't give her the reinforcement which would make her want to behave this way. When she reacts in what he considers to be her cool and aloof way he might become abusive and accuse her of anything from frigidity to unfaithfulness. If he were to receive the affection he wanted then he'd stop reacting with such hostility. And if he were to provide her with the reinforcement she required in the first place, then she would undoubtedly respond to him with affection and desire. But since, in this case, he doesn't have the insight to know how to go about getting what he needs, we're left with a 'I'll stop beating you if you'll be nice to me' stalemate, which reinforces the unhappiness of both partners. Time and again we see this kind of faulty communication in rocky marriages. In this case, the husband has tried to coerce the wife into giving him what he wants, and she is having none of it.

If coercion fails to produce any solutions, so does withdrawal. If one spouse withdraws socially or emotionally from the other, that other spouse will usually find other sources of reinforcement in the form of a lover, alcohol, even drugs.

In unhappy marriages each partner needs reinforcement from the other, but each is unwilling to provide it. Both need to be willing to break new ground in reinforcing the other, but often each is reluctant to take the first step. It is the job of the therapist, then, to break the deadlock and wean the marriage partners of their childish and naive behaviour.

Spelling it out
Stuart's practical approach to this task is easily described. Each spouse is asked to list three types of behaviour he or she would like the other partner to demonstrate more frequently.

The list has to be specific. A man can't say that he wants his wife to be more 'feminine' unless he states specifically what type of feminine behaviour he would like to see. Similarly, it is not enough for a wife to say that she wants her husband to be more 'sociable'. She would have to say, for example, that she wants him to talk to her at breakfast instead of reading the paper, that she wants to go out to dinner at least once a week instead of watching so much television, or that she wants to invite friends in for a drink at least once a month.

Once both partners have decided on three specific things they would like their mate to do differently, they post the list and then record how often they each do what's suggested on the list. This way they establish a base line for what I call their 'pre-therapy' behaviour. Then they can begin to give each other points for doing what was asked of them, each trying to match the other's score, in an arrangement best described as 'you scratch my back, and I'll scratch yours'. Crude and manipulative as this may seem, it works. Couples who previously had trouble expressing themselves to each other suddenly find that they are communicating in a fresh way, that they are finally getting what they need, even though the method is almost embarrassingly obvious. They have finally found a way to create reciprocal positive reinforcement.

One of the most common complaints among people in troubled relationships is that they feel that their partner should *know* what they want, and instinctively provide it. What a mistake this is. Even the most intelligent, sensitive people are not clairvoyant, and often people don't even know what they want themselves. It is very important, therefore to figure out what it is you want and need, and communicate it clearly to your partner.

Stuart's methods were rather primitive, as any pioneering venture usually is, but they provided a start in setting up healthy channels of communication in blocked relationships. Most of the reciprocal reinforcement in his experiments seemed to revolve around a sex-for-talk bargain – the women felt that they could be sexier and more loving with their husbands if their husbands would take the time to find out how they were feeling by talking to them more. Both partners, then, were seeking more intimacy. For the men it was sexual, for the women, verbal.

New developments in marital therapy

Since Stuart's early work only fifteen years ago huge strides have been made in helping people get along better through behavioural techniques. Many of these innovative procedures are discussed in *Marital Therapy: Strategies Based on Social Learning and Behavior Exchange Principles* by Neil Jacobson and Gayla Margolin. They conclude that the most important goal in marital counselling is to get couples to increase their positive exchanges, that is, to provide positive reinforcements for each other. Many marriages, they feel, suffer from 'reinforcement erosion', because the partners are so used to each other that they no longer excite each other the way they used to. In psychological jargon this tendency is called 'satiation' or 'habituation' and it is the process at work in the Coolidge Effect which I talked about earlier. So, to overcome this gradual loss of satisfaction in marriage, the partners have to make a real effort to find new positive reinforcers and to use them often with their spouse.

It is easier to increase positive reinforcers than to get rid of negative ones, so therapists tend to concentrate more on teaching spouses new ways of pleasing each other than on helping them stop old annoying ones. Jacobson and Margolin have set up a series of guidelines for making a marriage happier and they are worth thinking about. In helping a couple repair a sagging marriage two stages are necessary: first, diagnosis; second, treatment.

Diagnosis

When it comes to diagnosis, both partners must be taught that they are facing a problem together, and that the problem calls

for a *functional* not an emotional solution. They then have to discuss which behaviours in their spouse they hate and which they like. This is not to be done in a critical way; the point of it is not to punish the spouse but simply to make him as her aware of it. For example, the wife should be encouraged to avoid making her complaint accusingly, thus 'I hate the way you start watching television right after dinner, and let me do all the cleaning up, especially since I've gone to so much trouble to cook a terrific dinner for you.' Obviously this will make the husband angry and his reaction will be negative. A better way for her to put this complaint would be: 'I really appreciate the

way you have been helping me around the house lately, it's made all the difference in the world to me. There's just one little thing that bothers me, and that is that you don't do much to help me clean up after dinner.' This way the husband is apt to feel good about what he has been doing, and to give some serious thought to doing even more.

Teaching couples to present their case in a rational rather than emotional way, and to work through praise rather than criticism, is sometimes called 'social skills training', and much of marital counselling is involved with teaching couples to do just this. Sometimes role-playing helps, that is, getting the husband to play the part of the wife and vice versa. Alternatively, the therapist will make a video tape of a conversation between the couple and play it back to them so they can see more objectively how they interact. These social skills are very important and couples are encouraged to use them with other people, too, so that, often, as a result of effective therapy a person's whole life will perk up.

Step two in the diagnosis stage is insisting that the partner make his or her complaint very specific. Rather than a statement like 'you don't seem to be at all interested in what I do', it should be couched in terms such as 'When you get home from the office at night I'd like you to ask me what I did that afternoon.'

Step three requires that the partner drop all derogatory implications from his complaint. Not only is it not helpful to accuse the other person of being lazy, hostile or inconsiderate – it often produces the very kind of behaviour complained about. A husband may not be paying enough attention to his wife because of some crisis in his office, or because he's having trouble finishing his novel, or because he's coming down with the 'flu. If his wife starts berating him for being cold and uncaring, an even colder and more uncaring reaction is likely to ensue. Rather, she should state clearly and unaccusingly that she cares about him very much and she is concerned because he seems to be troubled by something.

The fourth guideline in the diagnosis stage says that the spouse who is complaining should admit to his or her role in the problem. Few problems are all the fault of one person. An example given by Jacobson and Margolin first describes the way the problem should *not* be stated. The wife says, 'I think you should spend more time playing with Linda.' The husband replies, 'I play with Linda more than you do, and besides when I do play with her you always interfere.' This is a typical defensive reaction that often follows a direct and one-sided accusation. What if the wife had stated her case this way: 'I know that I sometimes interfere when you are playing with Linda and I'd love to try to do something about this because I know it annoys you and I'd really like for you to play with her more.' Since the wife has admitted that they are both at fault, she is much more likely to get a positive response from her husband. He might say something like, 'You're right, I'm not spending enough time with her these days, and I'd like to do something about that.'

The fifth and final guideline says that the partner should state his complaint or complaints as briefly as possible. This is so that the couple should be encouraged, not to dwell on past problems, but to move swiftly forward in an attempt to solve their difficulties. Lengthy statements tend to have emotional overtones that are often negative. Raking up painful memories is not the point here. Getting on with solutions is.

Solution

Now that the diagnosis is complete and presented in the most positive and effective way, Jacobson and Margolin turn their attention to trying to work out a solution. Once again they offer several guidelines which may be useful to couples trying to work out their problems as well as to the therapists who are trying to help them.

Their first suggestion is to discuss only one problem at a time. Anyone who has ever had a fight with a spouse or lover knows how easy it is for a quarrel to escalate until suddenly it is open season on every aspect of the relationship. Obviously this is a very destructive way of going about things, and should be avoided at all costs.

The next piece of advice is that, when one of the spouses makes a statement or registers a complaint, the other should immediately reply by paraphrasing it. This shows that he or she has understood what the partner has said, and it implies that he or she is eager to find out more about what is bothering the spouse.

Suggestion number three is that the partner should not make inferences but talk only about actual observed behaviour. This prevents the kind of misinterpretation of intention that we talked about before.

The fourth suggestion is: 'Be neutral rather than negative.' Jacobson and Margolin say that 'When couples are fighting rather than collaborating, their interaction is frequently punctuated by attempts to put down, humiliate, or intimidate the partner. Such power struggles constitute the antithesis of problem solving. As such, their presence serves as a clear indication that at least one partner is really more interested in winning a battle than problem solving.' So, it is very important to avoid negative statements that belittle the partner in any way, and to stick to factual, neutral statements about what's bothering you.

The fifth suggestion is to focus on solutions. When we get to this stage, if there is a therapist present he will restate the problem in the most neutral language possible and then ask the two partners to suggest possible solutions. Brain storming is the best way to arrive at possible solutions. This means that the couples are asked to come up with as many solutions to the problem as they can think of, no matter how stupid they may sound at first. Absurd solutions are actually welcomed, because it becomes easier to eliminate various solutions without hurting the feelings of the person who made them. All possible solutions are written down by the therapist and then discussed in detail by the two partners.

From this discussion we come to the sixth and final suggestion, which is that 'Behaviour changes should include mutuality and compromise.' If the agreed-upon solution favours one or the other of the partners it won't work in the long run, so a good therapist will make sure that both partners will get what they need.

A contract for change

Once the couple have reached this agreement, what's next? Silly as it may sound, it is essential that the solution be spelled out down to the tiniest little detail. For example, the agreement might say that the husband will come home from Monday to Friday by 6.30 p.m. If for some reason he can't do this on a particular night he will have to let the wife know about it by 4.30, and at that time he'll tell her when he will be home. This is much better than an agreement which says that he will come home at a reasonable time, because what's reasonable is open to interpretation, and you can be sure that they each have a different idea on the subject. The agreement should be in writing and posted in a place where each can see it frequently.

This little piece of paper is what behaviourist marriage counsellors call a behaviour-change contract. It is sometimes called a contingency contract, because it makes changes in one partner's behaviour contingent on changes in the other partner's behaviour. Recently, behavioural therapists have developed another kind of contract – the good-faith contract – in which each partner makes an undertaking to change behaviour which does not depend on the other partner giving something in return. Certainly, not all therapists use contracts between the partners to help ailing marriages, but such contracts, when used, have been found to be extremely effective.

Is behavioural therapy the answer to problem marriages?

So now that we have taken a look at what I consider to be some of the most effective ways of helping distressed marriages, what are we to make of them? Many readers will probably react

negatively. What about love, what about spontaneity, what about romance? Or they may see the whole procedure as grossly oversimplified, treating people as if they were robots, rather than sensitive human beings. My answer to this kind of criticism is that this method may be flawed, imperfect, but very often it works. In my experience it works better than any other theory designed to modify human behaviour and, simplistic as it may seem, if the method helps save marriages as it clearly has and does, then why not embrace it? No one would deny that techniques of reward and reinforcement work in training animals. Is our evolutionary history not linked with other animals? Do our animal ancestors not show types of behaviour which we find in humans, from pair-bonding and monogamous love relationships, to polygyny and polyandry? True, we have socialized some of these animal drives and emotions, but not others, and the conflict between socialized behaviour on the one hand and the more primitive, instinctive behaviour on the other, can cause great tension in marriage. If it is possible to harness and redirect some of this potentially antisocial instinctive behaviour, as behaviourists try to do with their positive reinforcement techniques, then why not go with it? Until we come up with something better, why not make the best use of what we know to be effective? A good marriage is imperative to the happiness of most people. If yours happens to be in trouble I can't emphasize enough how important I think it is for you to try out some of these positive reinforcement methods. As I've said, several times before, silly or manipulative as they may seem, they get results.

Does therapy work?

If a marriage is breaking up, can marriage guidance help? Not as much as desperate couples on the brink of divorce might hope, according to an American study which was published in 1980. The author interviewed 124 men and women within two months of their divorce, 10 per cent of whom sought help from their local Marriage Guidance Council. Of the latter group, most admitted that they had been disappointed. They had regarded calling in such a agency as a last-ditch attempt to keep a doomed marriage away from the rocks, were looking for practical advice and claimed to have received none. 'They couldn't give advice or weren't prepared to' was one fairly typical comment.

In response, the MGC counsellors pointed out that their training expressly discouraged them from giving cut-and-dried advice to couples on a single visit. No two couples had the same problems, said the counsellors: only after a series of sessions over a period of time would the problems specific to each couple be identified. Clearly, the services offered by the MGC could never meet the needs of couples in crisis who wanted immediate help.

Other studies, however, show more cause for optimism. Researchers went back to 320 former marital therapy clients five years after they had first sought help to see how their marriage had fared during the intervening years and found not only that many couples who might have split up had remained together, but that some forms of therapy were more helpful than others. After five years more than half (56 per cent) of the couples where both the husband and wife had been seen together were still married, while only 30 per cent of the couples where only one partner had sought help were still together.

Ref: J. Richard Cookerly, *Does Marital Therapy Do Any Lasting Good?*, Journal of Marital and Family Therapy, Oct. 1980.
A. Mitchel, *Marriage Guidance, New Society*, Vol 19 page 25.

Epilogue

What conclusions can we draw from our discussions? Well, one thing that we can be pretty sure of is that marriage is here to stay. It has been with us in one form or another since the beginning of recorded history and it is essential to the sense of well-being, of happiness, in the large majority of people. We have also seen that human beings are incredibly varied, in their behaviour, in their attitudes, and in their emotions, so that to work out who is most likely to be happily married to whom we must take these enormous individual differences into account.

These differences are grounded in biology, but they are also affected by environment. To best understand a person's behaviour we must think of him as a biosocial animal, and look at the influences both of his heredity and of the society he grew up in. All this is a roundabout way of saying that nothing works for everybody, and that when it comes to marriage, the positive ways in which partners interact are just as varied as the partners themselves.

Hereditary happiness

Heredity has a profound influence on our personality, our libido and our happiness in marriage, but I've tried to show that heredity is only half the story. While it can push us in a certain direction, other forces can change this direction decisively. It's true that what we bring to a marriage – in the way of a happy disposition, stability, generosity, empathy and unselfishness – plays an important part in determining whether or not the marriage will be a happy one. But we can do a lot to increase our chances of happiness in marriage by choosing a partner who is appropriate for us, and I've tried to give you enough information in the preceding chapters to help you decide who may be right for you. As for the old adage that opposites attract, well, that may be true in the short run, but if a man and a woman are too different it doesn't bode well for a happy long-term relationship. I feel that the more alike two people are the better, and the greater their chances for a lasting happiness.

Keeping a marriage going

Within the marriage bond itself, we can do much to keep the partnership on track, by paying attention to some of the guidelines I discussed in the last chapter. I described a certain kind of marital therapy for marriages in trouble, but the principles involved apply to healthy marriages too. Of course all close relationships go through tough times, but how we deal with these problems is what will determine the long-term satisfaction of ourselves and our partners. Married people should take the equity principle to heart. It is a fundamental law of nature that in order to receive positive reinforcement from someone we must give it to them. This enlightened selfishness can enormously improve the chances of a happy marriage.

Since marriage is the focal point of so many of our needs, wants, responsibilities and cooperative efforts, it will not be easily jettisoned: there is simply nothing which can take its place. Whether it's living together, the 'companionate mar-riage' which exists without the formal marriage contract, or legalized marriage itself, the advantages of this relationship so far outweigh the disadvantages that the future of the institution is absolutely secure.

Security vs. excitement

Within this marital partnership, of course, there are many conflicts and tensions. The major one is that between stability and novelty, the desire to dig a firm foundation in a long-lasting relationship, and the desire for new adventures and conquests. This contradiction is deeply embedded in our biological nature. In general, as we have seen, introverts tend more toward the stability end of the continuum, extraverts toward the novelty end. You see this in the sexual as well as the social

211

aspect of relationships, and it must not be overlooked as a source of potential friction in marriage.

No easy solutions

I didn't write this book to supply oversimplified recipes, or magic formulas for solving the very complex problems created by intimate human relationships. I simply wanted to tell you what psychologists and social scientists know from their experimental studies about marriage and the factors contributing to a happy marriage. I hope to have given you enough information to help you see which type of person you are in terms of personality and attitudes, and then to be able to apply some of these findings into your own life. There are no general solutions that apply across the board. Our individuality is precious, but we must also learn that this individuality causes problems. Social science may help us to learn to live with these problems and maybe even to solve some of them, but it offers no universal solutions and shouldn't be blamed for failing to do so. All it can do is disclose the facts as they exist. Recognizing these facts is the beginning of wisdom.

References

Introduction

Charles, R. & Peel, J. *Equalities and Unequalities* London: Academic Press, 1973

Eysenck, H. J. *Sex and Personality* London: Open Books, 1976

Eysenck, H. J. 'Personality, marital satisfaction, and divorce' *Psychological Reports*, 1980, 47, 1235–1238

Eysenck, H. J. & Wakefield, J. A. 'Psychological factors as predictors of marital satisfaction' *Advances in Behaviour Research and Therapy*, 1981, 3, 151–192

Eysenck, H. J. & Wilson, G. D. *The Psychology of Sex* London: Dent. 1979

Murstein, B. J. *Love, Sex and Marriage through the Ages* New York: Springer, 1974

Thornes, B. & Collard, J. *Who Divorces?* London: Routledge & Kegan Paul, 1979

Wilson, G. D. *Love and Instinct* London: Temple Smith, 1981

Wilson, G. D. & Nias, D. *Love's Mysteries: The Psychology of Sexual Attraction* London: Open Books, 1976

Chapter 1

Burgess, E. W. & Cottrell, L. S. *Predicting Success or Failure in Marriage* New York: Prentice-Hall, 1939

Carter, H. & Glick, P. C. *Marriage and Divorce: A Social and Economic Study* Cambridge, Mass: Harvard University Press, 1976

Chester, R. & Peel, J. (Eds) *Equalities and Inequalities in Family Life* London: Academic Press, 1973.

Cooper, D. *The Death of the Family* London: Penguin Press, 1971

Dewsbury, D. P. 'Effects of novelty on copulatory behaviour: The Coolidge Effect and related phenomena' *Psychological Bulletin*, 1981, 89, 464–482.

Dominion, J. *Marriage in Britain 1945–1980* London: Study Commission on the Family, 1981

Gover, G. *Sex and Marriage in England Today* London: Nelson, 1971

Levinger, G. & Moles, O. C. (Eds) *Divorce and Separation: Context, Causes and Consequences* New York: Basic Books, 1979

Locke, H. J. *Predicting Adjustment in Marriage: A Comparison of a Divorced and a Happily Married Group* New York: Holt, 1951

Mitchell, G. *Behavioural Sex Differences in Nonhuman Primates* New York: Van Nostrand Reinhold, 1979

Moroney, R. H. *The Family and the State: Considerations for Social Policy* London: Longman, 1976

Mueller, C. W. & Page, H. 'Marital Instability: A study of its transmission between generations' *Journal of Marriage and the Family*, 1977, 38, 83–92

Murstein, B. I. *Who Will Marry Whom?* New York: Springer, 1976

Pearlin, J. 'Status Inequality and Stress in Marriage' *American Sociological Review*, 1975, 40, 344–357

Rimmer, L. *Families in Focus: Marriage, Divorce and Family Patterns* London: Study Commission on the Family, 1981

Stone, L. *The Family, Sex and Marriage in England 1500–1800* London: Weidenfeld & Nicolson, 1977

Terman, L. M. *Psychological Factors in Marital Happiness* New York: McGraw-Hill, 1938

Thornes, B. & Collard, J. *Who Divorces?* London: Routledge & Kegan Paul, 1979

Zuckerman, S. *The Social Life of Monkeys and Apes* London: Routledge & Kegan Paul, 1981

Chapter 2

Andrews, F. M. & Withey, S. B. *Social Indication of Well-Being* New York: Plenum, 1976

Bernard, J. *The Failure of Marriage* New York: Bantam Books, 1972

Bradburn, N. M. *The Structure of Psychological Well-Being* Chicago: Aldine, 1969

Bradburn, N. M. & Caplovitz, D. *Reports on Happiness* Chicago: Aldine, 1965

Campbell, A., Converse, P. E. & Rodgers, W. *The Quality of American Life* New York: Russell Sage Foundation, 1976

Glenn, N. D. 'The contribution of marriage to the psychological well-being of males and females' *Journal of Marriage and the Family*, 1975, 37, 594–600

Glenn, N. D. & Weaver, C. N. 'A note on family situation and global happiness' *Social Forces*, 1979, 57, 961–967

Glenn, N. D. & Weaver, C. 'The contribution of marital happiness to global happiness' *Journal of Marriage and the Family*, 1981, 43, 161–168

Howard, J. W. & Ewes, R. M. 'Linear prediction of marital happiness' *Personality and Social Psychology Bulletin*, 1976, 2, 478–480

Taylor, C. C. 'Marriages of Twins to Twins' *Acta Genet. Med. Gemellol.*, 1971, 20, 96–113

Chapter 3

Byrne, D. *The Attraction Paradigm* New York: Academic Press, 1971

Dean, G. & Gurak, D. T. 'Marital homogamy the second time around' *Journal of Marriage and the Family*, 1978, 40, 559–570

Eysenck, H. J. 'Personality, premarital sexual permissiveness and assortative mating' *Journal of Sex Research*, 1974, 10, 47–51

Eysenck, H. J. & Wakefield, J. A. 'Psychological factors as predictors of marital satisfaction' *Advances in Behaviour Research and Therapy*, 1981, 3, 151–192

Hill, M. S. 'Hereditary influence on the normal personality using the MMPI: Prospective assortative mating' *Behavior Genetics*, 1973, 3, 225–233.

Hunt, M. *Sexual Behaviour in the 1970s* Chicago: Playboy Press, 1974

Locke, H. J. *Predicting Adjustment in Marriage: A Comparison of a Divorced and a Happily Married Group* New York: Henry Holt, 1951

Nielsen, J. 'Mental Disorders in married couples (assortative mating)' *British Journal of Psychiatry*, 1964, 110, 683–697

Taylor, P. A. & Glenn, N. D. 'The utility of education and attractiveness for females' status attainment through marriage' *American Sociological Review*, 1976, 41, 484–498

Watkins, M. P. & Meredith, W. 'Spouse similarity in newly weds with respect to specific cognitive abilities, socioeconomic status, and education' *Behavior Genetics*, 1981, 11, 21

Vandenberg, S. G. 'Assortative mating, or who marries whom?' *Behavior Genetics*, 1972, 2, 127–157

Wilson, G. & Nias, D. *Love's Mysteries: The Psychology of Sexual Attraction* London: Open Books, 1976

Zonderman, A. B., Vandenberg, S. G., Spuhler, K. & Fain, P. R. 'Assortative marriage for cognitive abilities' *Behavior Genetics*, 1977, 7, 261–271

Chapter 4

Bentler, P. M. & Newcomb, M. D. 'Longitudinal study of marital success or failure' *Journal of Consulting and Clinical Psychology*, 1978, 46, 1053–1070

Burgess, E. W. & Cottrell, L. S. *Predicting Success or Failure in Marriage* New York: Prentice-Hall, 1939

Cattell, R. B. & Nesselbroade, J. R. 'Likeness and complementarity theories examined by sixteen personality factor measures on stably and unstably married couples' *Journal of Personality and Social Psychology*, 1967, 7, 351–361

Eysenck, H. J. *The Psychology of Politics* London: Routledge & Kegan Paul, 1954

Eysenck, H. J. 'Personality, marital satisfaction, and divorce' *Psychological Reports*, 1980, 47, 1235–1238

Eysenck, H. J. & Wakefield, J. A. 'Psychological factors as predictors of marital satisfaction' *Advances in Behaviour Research and Therapy*, 1981, 3, 151–192

Eysenck, H. J. & Wilson, G. D. (Eds) *The Psychological Basis of Ideology* Lancaster: MTP, 1978

Locke, H. J. *Predicting Adjustment in Marriage: A Comparison of a Divorced and a Happily Married Group* New York: Henry Holt, 1951

Murstein, B. I. *Who will marry whom?* New York: Springer, 1976

Prodöhl, D. *Gelingen und Scheitern ehelicher Partnerschaft* Zürich: Hogrefe, 1979

Szopinsky, J. 'Personality and the marriage bond' *Personality and Individual Differences*, 1980, 1, 93–94

Terman, L. M. *Psychological Factors in Marital Happiness* New York: McGraw-Hill, 1938

Thornes, B. & Collard, J. *Who Divorces?* London: Routledge & Kegan Paul, 1979

Zaleski, Z. 'Psychoticism and marital satisfaction' *Personality and Individual Differences*, 1981, 2, 245–246

Zaleski, Z. & Galkowska, M. 'Neuroticism and marital satisfaction' *Behaviour Research and Therapy*, 1978, 16, 285–286

Chapter 5

Byrne, D., Cherry, F., Lamberth, J. & Mitchell, H. E. 'Husband–wife similarity in response to erotic stimuli' *Journal of Personality*, 1973, 41, 385–395

Chilton, B. Psychosexual development in twins' *Journal of Biosocial Science*, 1972, 4, 277–286

Cooper, A. J. 'Some personality factors in frigidity' *Journal of Psychosomatic Research*, 1969, 13, 149–155

Costa, P. T. & McCrae, R. R. 'Influence of extraversion and neuroticism on subjective well-being in happy and unhappy people' *Journal of Personality and Social Psychology*, 1980, 38, 668–678

Eysenck, H. J. *Sex and Personality* London: Open Books, 1976

Eysenck, H. J. & Eysenck, S. B. G. *Psychoticism as a Dimension of Personality* London: Hodder & Stoughton, 1976; New York: Carne & Russak. 1977

Eysenck, H. J. & Wakefield, J. A. 'Psychological factors as predictors of marital satisfaction' *Advances in Behaviour Research and Therapy*, 1981, 3, 151–192

Giese, H. & Schmidt, A. *Studenten Sexualität* Hamburg: Rowohlt, 1968

Gorer, G. *Sex and Marriage in England Today* London: Nelson, 1971

Gothman, J. M. *Marital Interaction: Experimental Investigations* New York: Academic Press, 1979

Martin, N. G., Eaves, L. J. & Eysenck, H. J. 'Genetical, environmental and personality factors influencing the age of first sexual intercourse in twins' *Journal of Biosocial Science*, 1977, 9, 91–97

Reiss, I. L. *The Social Context of Premarital Sexual Permissiveness* New York: Holt, Rinehart & Winston, 1967

Schofield, M. *The Sexual Behaviour of Young People* London: Longmans, 1965

Schofield, M. *The Sexual Behaviour of Young Adults* London: Allen Lane, 1973

Sigurt, V., Schmidt, G., Rheinfeld, S. & Weidemann-Sutor, I. 'Psycho-sexual stimulation: sex differences' *Journal of Sexual Research*, 1970, 6, 10–24

Terman, L. M. 'Correlates of orgasm adequacy in a group of 556 wives' *Journal of Psychology*, 1951, 32, 115–172

Thomas, D. R. 'Conservatism and premarital sexual experience' *British Journal of Social and Clinical Psychology*, 1975, 14, 195–196

Zuckerman, M. et al. 'What is the sensation seeker? Personality trait and experience correlates of the sensation seeking scales' *Journal of Consulting and Clinical Psychology*, 1972, 39, 308–321

Chapter 6

Beit-Hallahmi, B. & Rabin, A. I. 'The Kibbutz as a social experiment and as a child-rearing laboratory' *American Psychologist*, 1977, 532–541

Dobash, Q. & Dobash, R. *Violence against Wives* London: Open Books, 1980

Eysenck, H. J. & Wilson, G. D. *The Psychology of Sex* London: Dent, 1979

Goldberg, S. *The Inevitability of Patriarchy* London: Temple Smith, 1977

217

Maccoby, E. E. & Jacklin, C. N. *The Psychology of Sex Differences* London: Oxford University Press, 1975

Mead, M. *Male and Female: A Study of the Sexes in a Changing World* New York: William Morrow, 1967

Okin, S. M. *Women in Western Political Thought* London: Virago, 1980

Shazar, R. K. (Ed) *The Plough Woman* New York: Herzl Press, 1975

Spiro, M. E. *Gender and Culture: Kibbutz Women Revisited* Durham, North Carolina: Duke University Press, 1979

Tiger, L. & Shepher, J. *Women in the Kibbutz* New York: Harcourt Brace-Jovanovich, 1975

Wesley, F. & Wesley, C. *Sex-role Psychology* New York: Human Sciences Press, 1977

Chapter 7

Bush, F. A. *Human Sexuality in Four Perspectives* Baltimore: Johns Hopkins University Press, 1977

Campbell, B. (Ed) *Sexual Selection and the Descent of Man* Chicago: Aldine, 1972

Ciba Foundation Symposium. Sex, Hormones and Behaviour. Oxford: *Excerpta Medica*, 1979

Dorner, G. *Sexualhormonabhangige Gehirndifferenzierung und Sexualitat* New York: Springer-Verlag, 1972

Eysenck, H. J. & Wilson, G. D. *The Psychology of Sex* London: Dent, 1979

Fisher, S. *Understanding the Female Orgasm* Harmondsworth: Penguin, 1973

Gosselin, C. C. & Wilson, G. D. *Sexual Variation: Fetishism, Sado-Masochism and Transvestism* London: Faber & Faber, 1981

Gray, J. A. 'Sex differences in emotional behavior in mammals including man: Endocrine bases' *Acta Psychologica*, 1971, 35, 29–46

Haddon, C. *The Limits of Sex* London: Michael Joseph, 1982

Levine, S. (Ed) *Hormones and Behaviour* London: Academic Press, 1972

Mitchell, G. *Behavioral Sex Differences in Nonhuman Primates* New York: Van Nostrand Reinhold, 1979

Money, J. & Ehrhardt, A. A. *Man and Woman, Boy and Girl* Baltimore: Johns Hopkins University Press, 1972

Reinisch, J. M. 'Fetal hormones, the brain, and human sex differences: A heuristic, integrative review of the recent literature' *Archives of Sexual Behavior*, 1974, 3, 51–90

Schlegel, W. *Die Sexual instinkte des Menschen* Munich: Rutten Verlag, 1966

Symons, D. *The Evolution of Human Sexuality* London: Oxford University Press, 1979

Wilson, E. O. *Sociobiology: The New Synthesis* Cambridge, Mass.: Belknap, 1975

Wilson, G. D. *Love and Instinct* London: Temple Smith, 1981

Chapter 8

Ables, B. S. & Brandsma, J. M. *Therapy for Couples* San Francisco: Jossey-Bass, 1977

Crago, M. A. 'Psychopathology in married couples' *Psychological Bulletin*, 1972, 77, 114–128

Gelles, R. J. *The Violent Home: A Study of Physical Aggression Between Husbands and Wives* Beverly Hills: Sage, 1972

Gottman, J. M. *Marital Interaction* London: Academic Press, 1979

Jacobson, N. S. & Margolin, G. *Marital Therapy* New York: Brunner/Mazel, 1979

Kanfer, F. & Goldstein, A. P. (Eds) *Helping People Change* London: Pergamon, 1975

Knox, D. *Marriage and Happiness: A Behavioral Guide to Counselling* Champaign, Illinois: Research Press, 1971

Meichenbaum, D. H. *Cognitive Behavior Modification* New York: Plenum, 1977

Miunchin, S. *Families and Family Therapy* Cambridge, Mass: Harvard University Press, 1974

Olson, D. H. C. (Ed) *Treating Relationships* Lake Mills, Iowa: Graphic, 1976

Patterson, G. R. *Families: Applications of Social Learning to Family Life* Champaign, Illinois, Research Press, 1971

Sager, C. *Marriage Contracts and Couple Therapy* New York: Brunner/Mazel, 1976

Thomas, E. J. *Marital Communication and Decision-Making* New York: Free Press, 1977

Index

ILLUSTRATIONS